W9-CFA-747

To Ken
Your best

Ernst Teoff

Grant Teaff

with Margaret Leary

Coaching
IN THE
Classroom

TEACHING
SELF-MOTIVATION

CORD
COMMUNICATIONS

Copyright © 1994
Center for Occupational Research and Development, Inc.
All rights reserved

Reproduction or translation of any part of this work beyond
that permitted by Sections 107 and 108 of the 1976 United
States Copyright Act without the permission of the copyright
owner is unlawful. Requests for permission or further infor-
mation should be addressed to
   Permissions Department
   CORD Communications
   P.O. Box 21206
   Waco, Texas 76702-1206

ISBN 155502–557–9
Library of Congress Number 94–71927

Printed in the United States of America

Positive Power for Successful Salesmen copyright 1972 by
Droke House/Hallux

Ebony Magazine January 1992 by Johnson Publications

Lincoln on Leadership copyright 1992 by Warner Books

The teacher comments contained in this book were solic-
ited from them in group meetings and teleconferences.
Teachers were not paid for their participation in this
process.

The comments of the teachers do not necessarily reflect
the opinions of CORD or Grant Teaff, and their inclusion
in this book should not be construed as endorsement by
CORD or Grant Teaff.

Dedication

To Mrs. Stanfield, my second-grade teacher, who represents all those who coached me in the classroom in
elementary school and junior high school.

To Mrs. M. M. O'Rear, English teacher, who represents
all my high-school teachers.

To Vernie Newman, at McMurry College, who made
history come alive, and who represents all my college
professors.

And to Ann Miller, master teacher at Baylor University,
who represents all those great teachers through the
years who coached my own children and my players in
the classroom.

And finally, to all those teachers who largely go unrec-
ognized and are underpaid, but are committed and
dedicated to students and their education.

Acknowledgments

A special thanks to Margaret Leary who patiently urged me, in the midst of much going on, to get this manuscript completed. Her encouragement was invaluable.

To Teresa Lynn Teaff, my middle daughter, who is the Coordinator of Special Education in the Waxahachie School System (Texas) and one of the most outstanding teachers I have ever come in contact with. Her review of the manuscript, on a weekly basis, proved to be most helpful as she viewed it, not with the eye of a daughter, but with the eye of a teacher.

CONTENTS

PREFACE
Coaching and Teaching

I've always been fascinated by great classroom teachers. I used to question my own children about the experiences they were having in the classroom and I talked constantly to the hundreds of players I had through the years about *their* experiences in the classroom. I have asked individuals in all walks of life to describe the best teacher they have ever had. The description was always of a teacher who cared, who knew his or her subject matter and expanded on it, a teacher who had a disciplined classroom, and one who taught his or her students how to be self-motivated. Thinking back on the best classroom teachers I had, I discovered these teachers all had similar traits, and they all had high expectations of me. Comparing their traits with the descriptions I had gathered from others, I came to the conclusion that those master teachers were all *coaching* their students.

A classroom coach is innovative with the subject matter and always wants the students to develop their best traits, to set high goals, and to learn the basic principles of success that can be used in everyday life. A classroom coach develops a learning environment that eliminates hostility, criticism, condemnation, fear, appre-

1

hension, jealousy, and hate. A classroom coach is an encourager who uses praise, acceptance, love, and approval to build self-confidence and integrity. And finally a classroom coach is fair, just, and honest, creating a friendly environment.

In 1985, I wrote a book entitled *Winning*, which I dedicated to the coaches who had touched my life in one way or another. My high school coaches had inspired me to become a coach, my college coaches had taught me how to play the game of football. Some of the top track coaches in the state of Texas had shared their knowledge with me when I was an aspiring track coach. There were also those coaches who had seen something in me and given me an opportunity to advance in my chosen profession. In *Winning*, I also recognized the hundreds of high school coaches who had shared their knowledge with me as well as their players, and the many coaches who had worked with me and so faithfully shared my opportunities, my goals, and my philosophy. And finally, I dedicated the book to the men and women in our profession who are serving the youth of America now and will serve them in the future.

By that dedication, I publicly recognized the importance of coaches in my life and my chosen profession. I could just as easily have listed a group of teachers at all levels of my educational experience who impacted me in the same way. The common thread that connects the teachers and coaches who molded my life is that they all approached what they were doing with full knowledge of their subject matter and innovativeness in presenting the material. Above all, they did it in a manner which made me feel they cared about me personally. This somehow made me want to learn.

The majority of my adult life has been spent coaching football and track. The lion's share was spent coaching football. For three of the nine years I coached track at McMurry College in Abilene, Texas, I was an assistant football coach, and for six of the nine years, the head football coach. The experience I gained in coaching track has been invaluable to me as a football coach. The skills I learned there helped me in several different areas, one of which was how to help a group of individuals become a team. In team sports such as football, it's necessary for a group of people, often from radically different backgrounds, to learn to work together. These people have to rely on each other's skill to achieve the overall goals of the team. They have to do their own jobs as members of the team, and they must be able to understand the integral part each of them plays in the overall strategy that will enable them to reach the goal of winning games.

In many ways, the goals of coaching are similar to the goals of teaching. Most dedicated teachers, like coaches, are interested in teaching more than their subject matter. They're interested in helping their students succeed, both in academics and in life. They're interested in helping their students learn to work together, to communicate, to set goals, and to achieve those goals. They're deeply interested in generating a spark in their students that could change their lives forever.

It is important to realize that, as teachers and coaches, we are role models—whether we want to be or not. And as role models, we impact our students either negatively or positively.

A positive approach to teaching as well as a positive atmosphere in which students can best learn, are, interestingly enough, created for the most part by the teacher. Therefore I believe that, to be most effective, a teacher must begin with a positive attitude. If teachers can learn to approach life in a positive frame of mind, all other things will fall into place. So the first section of this book will be dedicated to the premise that as teachers and coaches, we must be at our best. To be at our best, we must recognize the potential in ourselves, then develop that potential.

I.
Personal Development

For you to be better tomorrow than today, you have to plan to be better. Any plan for improvement should include the intangible powers that we possess.

—Grant Teaff

'Kids don't really care how much you know until they know how much you care.' That's the slogan for our program for at-risk kids.

—Wally Green, high-school teacher,
Las Cruces, New Mexico

INTRODUCTION
Developing the Intangibles

An eighteenth-century English poet wrote, "The best is yet to be." When I first read these words, I was amazed that a person of great literary renown and a small-town West Texas country boy could have the same philosophy: *The best is yet to be.* The belief that a positive attitude allows us to look to tomorrow with a positive expectation is not exclusively the property of a literary genius or of a country boy aspiring to succeed. A positive attitude is common property, and can be acquired.

In other words, we as human beings are free to approach life as we want to.

Unfortunately, in the society in which we live today, so much is negative and there are so many visible problems that a high percentage of the people with whom we come in contact have a negative attitude. I don't think many of them have ever thought about the fact that they could change their attitude by controlling their thinking. Therefore, they maintain a natural, negative attitude.

When I was growing up I didn't know anything about computers, but I realized that everything I read, heard, or witnessed, affected the way I thought. After all, the human brain is nothing more than a computer. Like a computer, it is incapable of producing anything that has not been put in. Therefore, the simple premise of *what goes in, comes out*, is a key to having a positive attitude. What you put into your personal brain/computer comes out in terms of the way you approach life, and in the way you think. To change your attitude or your behavior patterns, you must put the right stuff into your brain/computer. You should control what you read, listen to, and watch, and be aware that those you choose to associate with will ultimately have a profound effect on who you become.

For you to be better tomorrow than today, you have to plan to be better. Any plan for improvement should include the intangible powers that we possess.

It's interesting that the majority of personal development hinges around those characteristics and qualities that you can't see, feel, or touch, but that are the difference-makers. I've always referred to these as the intangibles. Like you, your students possess these intangibles. Most of the time they are not recognized, and at best are underdeveloped. If you can recognize your own intangibles and develop them to the fullest, then you can do a better job of helping your students recognize and develop their intangibles and become the best they can be.

There are five basic intangibles: attitude, goals, determination, belief, and caring. Even if we're strong in these areas, we can still improve. And the better we get, the more productive we will be as teachers, coaches, husbands, wives, fathers, mothers—people.

1.
The Power of a Positive Attitude

Let's start with attitude. There are three basic attitudes: a positive attitude, a negative attitude, and an "I don't care either way" attitude. Since the latter is actually a negative attitude, in essence there are really only two—positive and negative—and that's what we will focus on. First, there is a need to recognize that a negative attitude is a losing attitude; a positive attitude is a winning attitude. Years ago there was a song with a very catchy tune that had in its lyrics, "accentuate the positive, eliminate the negative." I consider this an excellent plan: to magnify the positives in your life, and get rid of the negatives.

Remember, attitudes don't get bad overnight, nor do they change to the positive quickly. They are developed or adjusted rather than changed, and by using the theory "what goes in, comes back out," we can form a plan to consciously feed into our own brains only those things that are positive.

One of the techniques I've used for years to consciously eliminate negative thinking is to force myself to think positive thoughts. For example, "We are going to win this game," or "We are going to play well," or "Good things are going to happen to us today." Years ago I started to teach the players to visualize the good things that would happen in a game, thereby creating a positive expectation in their minds. Since the mind has the ability to create pictures, we can actually see ourselves doing certain things, performing certain acts, and if we think of ourselves as doing those acts in a positive way—acting successfully— and visualize ourselves triumphant, it fills us with a strong sense of positiveness.

Every summer for years I have conducted the Grant Teaff Football Camp. It's for eight- to twelve-year-olds, and I like to teach the little guys everything I teach the big guys. Sometimes I have some interesting results. A few years ago on the first night of our camp, I told the youngsters that I was going to teach them how to think positively. I gave them this instruction: "All day tomorrow, I want you to consciously eliminate your negative thoughts. Here's what you do. Be aware when you have a negative thought and count each one of them. Tomorrow night I will ask each of you how many negative thoughts you had, and it will be interesting to see which one of you has the fewest."

The next night I started our meeting by asking every boy who had had ten or more negative thoughts to raise his hand. A high percentage of the boys raised their hands. Then I asked if anyone had had less than five negative thoughts. Three hands went up. Then I asked if anyone had gone through the day without one negative thought. To my amazement, one hand went up. It was that of 10-year-old J. J. Cox.

I said, "J. J., you went through the whole day without a negative thought?"

Obviously quite proud, he said loudly, "Yes, sir."

I told him I was very happy for him and asked the group to applaud. They did, since they were impressed as well.

Later, after the meeting, I was talking to a group of

boys when I felt a tug on my belt. It was J. J. With a puzzled look on his face, he asked softly, "Coach, what's a negative thought?"

The point was very clear to me. It's important to know what negative thoughts are if you want to eliminate them. It takes a good deal of practice to identify your thought patterns as negative, and even more practice to eliminate them.

Developing a positive attitude takes effort and concentration. Your attitude must be set each and every day. People who know me describe me as a person with a positive attitude, and rightly so. I have a positive attitude, but the secret is that I don't wake up each morning with that positive attitude. I have to develop it. I have to set the mood for the day, and to do this I use a technique that is simple and effective. I'll share it with you. Since my brain/computer understands English, I say some very simple English words. As I speak these words, I think about them and am filled with a very positive feeling. My attitude for the day is now set. The words I repeat every day are these:

> I am only one, but I am one.
> I cannot do everything, but I can do
> something.
> That which I can do, I ought to do.
> And that which I ought to do, I will do.

Even writing these words fills me with a very strong sense of positiveness. I have conditioned myself to respond to them, and I immediately feel my outlook brighten and my attitude become clearer and sharper toward the good things that are going to happen. The reason is that, in this vastly overpopulated world, I am only one and I recognize that. But the beautiful part is that I am one. I am an individual created to be distinctly different, and that makes me very special.

I recognize that I can't do everything. Sometimes we get caught up in so many responsibilities and jobs that we feel pulled apart and it affects us in a negative way. We have to realize that we can't do everything. However we can do something. And that which we can do, we have a responsibility to do. If we can do it, we ought to do it.

The first time I shared this particular grouping of words with a team was at Angelo State University in 1968. We were going to play the defending national champion, Texas A&I, who was a three-touchdown favorite. A lot of bad things had happened to our team during the season, and going into the game the players did not have a positive expectation. So I discussed with them the positive thoughts that were embodied in this statement. We concluded with "that which I can do, I will do," which in essence is a commitment to use our individual talents and ability. As I looked around the room, I saw the head of one of our players moving up and down, nodding in affirmation. That young man was a sophomore tailback from Lubbock, Texas, named Jerry Austin. Jerry didn't have great speed, but he had unusual physical toughness and the ability to keep his feet. When I saw Jerry nodding his head, I knew that we needed to give him the ball during the game…many times.

We were not a strong passing team. But Jerry Austin gave us the ability to be a good running team, because he was a strong physical runner. With Jerry's affirmation, the plan emerged in everyone's mind: We will run the ball. That which we can do, we will do.

Run the ball we did, and Jerry was outstanding.

The Angelo State Rams played the best game of the year. Upsetting the defending national champions, Jerry Austin epitomized the team's resolve to take a positive approach, doing what we were capable of doing: running the football. Instead of trying to force the square peg into the round hole and do something we weren't capable of doing, we just zeroed in on what we could do. It was a great lesson and a great victory.

So, when you get up in the morning, repeat those positive words. If, during the day, you have a sinking spell, stop, reload your mind—refill the computer—with the positive thoughts contained in them.

A group of secondary school teachers agreed to be involved in a discussion of how they coach in the classroom.

"As to having a positive attitude," said JoAnn Snider of Wynne, Arkansas, "I agree that it is essential, but let me tell you, some days it's almost more than I can do. Sometimes my students are so apathetic, I ask myself what I'm doing here. But then I make myself analyze the situation and say, 'These are the good things about this situation, and these are the bad things. I'm going to see what I can work on to make it better.' But it's hard sometimes to find something that's positive."

"I think one of the biggest things I have to combat in my students is the 'I don't care' attitude they have," said Cheryl Powell, of Plainview, Texas.

"The attitude my kids often have is 'It doesn't really matter to me,'" said Cindy Witt, of Mt. Vernon, Kentucky. "So I have to try and tie whatever concept I'm teaching them to their own lives somehow. I agree that attitudes don't change overnight. They're not like switches that can be turned on and off."

"I agree," said Otis Prater, of Berea,

Kentucky. "The attitude I find—and I teach General Science, a freshman course—is a generally negative attitude. And I think it really comes from the parents. A lot of the one-parent families really struggle, and it's hard for them to keep a positive attitude. The way I try to combat this is to find something positive to say to a student every day. Sometimes I really have to stretch to find it, but I always do.

"I think we need to teach the students to develop a positive attitude. One thing I think our school does right is that, in our summer-school session, we actually have motivational speakers come in and work on setting goals and developing a positive attitude. Some summers, one day a week is spent with our former graduates who are now in college or other post-secondary educational institutes talking to students about these issues. It's often more effective to have people closer to their age talking to the students about the value of setting goals and having a positive attitude. I wish we did it more with the students in regular school sessions."

2.
The Power of Influence

When I was a child I was influenced by almost everyone I came in contact with. I was certainly influenced by my parents in a profound way, but others had an impact on me, too: coaches, teachers, men and women in the community, individuals I came to know through my church, and even my peers. We all have role models and are influenced by them.

I coached for thirty-six years. The reason I decided at a very early age to become a coach was that I was influenced. I was impacted, and my life was changed, by my high-school coaches. They influenced me to want to do the same thing for others. Now to do that, I was influenced to begin setting goals. In order to get somewhere, you have to know where you're going. And then to get there, you have to work at it on a daily basis.

Just about everything that has developed my character, my attitude, my goals, and my ultimate ambitions, has been the influence of one or more individuals. For example, two sets of people influenced me to go to college and receive three degrees. First, my high-school coaches influenced me to want to become a coach, and I realized that I could not be a coach unless I got a college degree.

Second, in the oil fields west of Snyder in the summer after my senior year, I was employed as a roughneck on a drilling rig. It not only was the hardest work that I had ever done, it was by far the most dangerous. About halfway into that summer, I was influenced by the job itself and the guys I worked with, who had spent their entire life drilling for oil in one West Texas town after another, to choose not to spend my life on a drilling rig. Instead, I chose to get an education.

However, even when we're influenced to strive for certain goals, that doesn't mean everything is going to go smoothly. I had no aptitude for math and very little interest in it. In my sophomore year, I actually flunked a math course and thought my life had come to an end. When the reality of failure in that math course struck me, I found it very hard to keep a positive attitude. My thought line was simple: 'I'm going to flunk out of high school and I won't be eligible to play football next year, so why stay in school? If I can't play football, I should go ahead and join the army and try to make something out of myself.'

To me, even though I had been influenced to get a degree, I had failed, and would now miss out on that opportunity. In other words, I was ready to give up. Although I knew the importance of a positive attitude, my attitude quickly became negative. But thanks to the influence of a former coach, outstanding teacher, and businessman in Snyder, my life was put back on track. After failing the math course, I went to see Carl Herod to tell him what had happened, and what I was going to do.

I said, "Mr. Herod, I failed my math exam. I'm going to join the army and try to do something with my life."

He looked me in the eye and said, "Nonsense. Will you do what it takes to get the job done?"

I said, "I'll do anything."

He said, "That anything is being willing to study, listen, apply yourself, and pass the test."

I said, "I can't! I've already flunked it."

He said, "I'll call you in a little while."

Carl Herod happened to be a strong teacher in the area of math, and well respected. He went up to the school, talked to the principal and the math teacher, and I guess because of my behavioral pattern, because my teachers liked me, and because Mr. Herod was respected, they decided to give me one more chance to pass the math test. So Mr. Herod called me and said, "Do you still want to get a high-school education, go to college, and become a coach?"

I said, "Of course I do."

He said, "I'll meet you at your house at five this afternoon. Be ready to work."

That afternoon, Mr. Herod came in and sat down and started to teach me the math that I had failed to learn. He made it so simple, and he kept saying, "You can do it. There's no question about it. You can do it."

We studied for many hours, then the next day we came back and studied some more. On the third day, he said, "You're ready for the test."

With a smile on my face, I said, "I think I am, Mr. Herod, thanks to you."

We went to the school. The principal and the teacher laid out the test and I passed it with flying colors, thereby passing my course, and getting the opportunity to finish high school and to have a chance at eventually becoming a coach.

It still wasn't easy sailing. I wasn't big enough or fast enough in high school to get a scholarship to go to college. I felt I needed one and wanted to play because I thought it would make me a better coach in the future. Because my high-school coach, Speedy Moffat, knew my goals, he was willing to help. He drove me to the beautiful city of San Angelo, Texas, to meet with Max Bumgardner, the head coach of San Angelo College, a junior college.

Coach Moffat influenced Coach Bumgardner so that he was willing to give me a tryout. Personally, I was motivated to make the team, no matter what. Though too little and too slow, I was going to do whatever it took to get the job done.

When we started two-a-days, my effort, my positive attitude, and my determination gave me the chance to earn a scholarship. At 150 pounds, I became a starting linebacker. Just before school was about to start, Coach Bumgardner called me into his office and said, "A part of our scholarship is a part-time job. Besides playing football, you have to work to help earn your scholarship."

I said, "Fine."

Then he said, "Would you like to work at a radio station?"

I asked, "Why?"

Coach Bumgardner looked at me rather strangely, and said, "Well, you want to be a coach, don't you?"

The next day I reported to the radio station. This was an important step for me, and I began to realize why Coach Bumgardner had suggested it. Working in the communication field, I could learn to articulate. I could be influenced by people in radio and I could learn to be comfortable in front of a microphone. That in turn would help me to learn to communicate, and being able to communicate would give me a better chance to be a successful coach.

So I walked into the small radio station that afternoon, just seventeen years old. A thin man in a short-sleeved shirt was standing by the control room of the radio station and he motioned me to come to him. I walked up and introduced myself. He said, "Come on in. You're on the afternoon shift." He then proceeded to walk over to the console, which had a turntable on either side and more switches and knobs than I'd ever seen in my life, and began to explain to me how to cue up a record, and how to shut the mike off when I wasn't talking. He also showed me how to operate the "cough switch."

"If you're on the air and you need to cough," he said, "you hit this switch."

He showed me how to cue up the commercials, demonstrated how to count down on the clock, and said, "You have two radio shows this afternoon. Come with me and I'll help you pick out the records."

I'd said virtually nothing up to this point, but now I asked, "What kind of radio shows do I have?"

He smiled and said, "You have a classical show with classical music, and you have the *Eddie Arnold Show*. That one's easy," he said, "because you only play Eddie Arnold records."

My mind was racing, my eyes glazing over. I was going to go on the air twenty minutes after walking into a radio station. Now you've got to remember: I'm from West Texas, where we talk slow, and, some people think, a little funny. I've often wondered what went through the mind of the music professors there at the junior college who heard my first broadcast and tried to recognize the names of the artists and the music I stumbled to pronounce during my opening show. However ineptly, my career in radio had begun.

While pursuing my education at San Angelo College and then at McMurry College in Abilene, I continued to work in radio and, later, in television. As a senior in college, I not only worked on my master's degree and played football, but I also worked full time at the local television station. I was driven and consumed by my goal to be totally prepared to become a college coach.

My coach and teacher Mule Kizer was a great influence on me. He not only taught me how to play the game of football, but assured me that it was okay to like poetry, classical music, and literature. Being a hard-nosed football player is just a small part of life, he told me. Coach Kizer is still a great influence on me. In his late eighties now, he's off somewhere in the Andes, exploring and writing poetry. I just received his latest about a week ago.

"We teachers are probably the most positive and constant influence some of our students have," said Sharon Rondone, of Cherry Valley, Arkansas. "Even the kids who have good parents often have parents who are separated or divorced. And when it's a split home, there's going to be conflict. We are able to provide an environment where that conflict is not there.

"People who think teachers work only nine months out of the year don't realize that we really work about eighteen hours a day for those nine months. When we're not with our kids, they're often on our minds. We work with them; we think about them constantly; we call their parents. And it's good to remember that we really are their role models. Sometimes I get so bogged down in the everyday tasks that I forget that, but the kids remember things that we say and do for years afterward.

"Some of my kids live in one-parent families, and often the one parent has to work two jobs to support the household. That means that the child often leaves an empty home and returns to an empty home. You can't blame the parent, but who is going to meet the child's emotional needs? More and more, it's the teacher. And that's what burns the good teachers out."

"I agree," said JoAnn. "I have the same situation as Sharon. Many of my students have a lot of emotional needs, and it's not just in the one-parent families. In many two-parent families, both parents work and the student still leaves or returns to an empty house. Who's there to talk to them? Who asks them how their day

went? Often, it's no one. By the time the parents come home, they're too tired to do much but eat and sit in front of the television. Often, no one asks the kids what they want to do with their lives, no one encourages them to do well in school.

"I believe that the breakdown of the American family is what has changed the face of America and the burden of teaching, and we're already paying a high price. Kids need to be given rules. They need love and attention. They need someone to be interested in them. And often, their teacher is the only one who is. God help them if they get a teacher who believes in teaching only from 8.30 a.m. to 3.30 p.m., and having no other involvement with his or her students."

I found a poem years ago whose author is unknown. But the poem sums it all up, pointing out very clearly that each of us is influencing someone else, whether we want to or not.

Influence

There are little eyes upon you,
And they're watching night and day;
There are little ears that quickly
Take in every word you say;
There are little hands all eager
To do anything you do;
And a little boy who's dreaming
Of the day he'll be like you.

There's a wide-eyed little fellow,
Who believes you're always right,
And his ears are always open,

And he watches day and night;
You are setting an example
Every day in all you do,
For the little boy who's waiting
To grow up to be like you.

Like the little boy, I've been influenced by others, and I'm fully aware that in everything I do I have an influence on someone else.

"Talking about influence," said Wally Green of Las Cruces, New Mexico, who teaches Applied Chemistry, Enriched Chemistry, and Biology, "let me tell you about a program that has really influenced some of our students. Our kids don't always want to be in the classroom. So we have to find ways to help them become motivated. About five years ago, I got involved in the Renaissance program (See Appendix), which is a program to encourage at-risk kids to stay in school. We structured the whole thing as we do in coaching.

"We give them stickers and other rewards that acknowledge achievement, but the underlying philosophy of the program is that kids don't really care how much you know until they know how much you care. *That's our slogan. Until you show the kids how much you care—and especially the at-risk kids—they're not going to care about what you want to teach them.*

"We spend a great deal of class time just having discussion about what's going on in the kids' lives. We have a lot of gangs, and it takes a long time to build up the students' trust, but by the second semester that they're in the

program, they're usually finally willing to open up about some of the stuff that's going on. The program's five years old now, and we've been able to keep a lot of kids in school through it. Although we do offer rewards and incentives, that's not what seems to matter most to the kids. What really seems to count is the attention they get from the teachers. They need that positive reinforcement."

"I agree," said David Griego, of Mora, New Mexico, a math and science teacher for grades 9-12. "I think that teachers can really influence kids a lot. Coaches spend a lot of time getting to know their players and being on a first-name basis with them. I think it's so important that teachers do the same. To get to know my students better, I use a club program called MESA (See Appendix). It's a math, engineering, and science achievement program. I get my students involved in competition, and I actually coach my students to get them ready for the competitions. I get to know the kids a lot better through that program, because I'm with them on field trips to various competitions throughout the state. I feel that because of this, I have a positive influence on the kids.

"MESA's goals are to involve minority students in areas like math and science where they have been traditionally underrepresented. I have fifty-two students involved in MESA at the moment, which is up from the seventeen I started with four years ago. The kids really like MESA. They like being able to have a teacher go with them to various places; they like the idea of the incentives the program provides for meeting its goals—attending meetings, being

involved in competitions, receiving high grades, and taking math and science each year. Corporate sponsors underwrite the cash incentives that MESA provides, and these allow students to win up to $1,000 each in the four years they are eligible for the program. The awards are not presented until graduation, and so are an incentive for students to set and meet long-term goals. Corporations realize that, after kids have been in the MESA program for four years, they form a pool of students with significant achievements who will be available to be recruited by the corporations.

"MESA has a very positive influence on our students."

Most folks are astounded to know that I knew when I was thirteen years old that I wanted to be a college coach. And most seem amazed when I tell them that I decided I wanted to coach on the college level because of the influence of one man. That man was Kern Tipps, a broadcaster for the Southwest Conference Radio Network, calling Southwest Conference (SWC) games as a play-by-play announcer. I would lie on the floor in front of our big radio, close my eyes, and listen to the vivid description of the game being played, and I could just see myself on the sideline coaching one of those great SWC schools. So I just started telling everybody I wanted to coach in the SWC. Evidently, my high-school friends believed me, because in our high-school senior annual there is a page called "Prophecies," where whoever did the prophesying said that Grant Teaff would be the head football coach at the University of Texas. Well, they missed it by about a hundred miles. But they didn't miss the fact that my goals were set to coach in the SWC. Why? Again, influence.

"I teach ninth and tenth graders," said JoAnn, who teaches Biology, Applied Biology, and Chemistry. "Because of the breakdown of the American family, more and more of the responsibility for the child's total development is falling on us, the teachers. We're sometimes the only people some of our students talk to during the day. In the last fifteen years, my students' need for stability and caring has increased dramatically. Students often want to come to my class simply because I've been around at the school a long time, and I represent something stable in their lives. I've also coached volleyball teams, and I'm the junior/senior sponsor. The kids know I care about them, and that seems to be what they respond to most. I know I influence them, so I guess it's up to me to help them figure out what they might want to do with their lives. I put quite a bit of emphasis on their setting goals."

3.
The Power of Goals

By the time I was in college, I had learned to set goals in all areas of my life. When I married Donell Phillips in 1956, the first thing I did was to sit down with her and explain the importance of goals in my life, and how we as a couple should set goals in every area—financial, physical, personal, and spiritual. We decided to work daily to reach all the goals we'd set. Our daily effort included writing down ways we could reach our goals and then prioritizing those different ways. In other words, each day we would be doing the most important things that would help us reach our goals.

Through small successes, Donell and I began to recognize the power of goals in our lives. The first success was very important to us. We only had $75.00 a month to spend on an apartment. We looked all over the city of Lubbock and couldn't find anything that was decent and within $20.00 of our allotted amount. But that $75.00 apartment was our goal, and we were going to reach it one way or another. After an exasperating week of looking in the newspapers, we decided to take matters into our own hands, and early one Saturday morning, we started driving the streets of Lubbock. About mid-afternoon, tired and weary, we were driving in the north part of Lubbock when Donell said, "Oh, look at that street! It's named Baylor Street. Baylor's a SWC school, and our goal is to end up in the Southwest Conference. Maybe we can find an apartment on this street." About halfway down the first block on the right-hand side was a very small apartment complex with a sign outside, "Apartment for Rent."

We pulled up to the door, got out, went in, and asked about the vacant apartment. The lady asked, "Would you like to see it?"

We walked behind her for about twenty paces and she opened the door into an apartment which was perfect. Nervously I asked, "How much is this apartment?"

She smiled and said, "It's $75, all bills paid."

For some reason, when Donell and I started setting goals, we decided to use three years as the target date for reaching them. So, any goal we set was to be based on a three-year cycle. As I look back now it is not only interesting, but almost mystifying, to see that we continue to reach our goals in three-year cycles.

When we married, I was coaching at Lubbock High School. Our goal, however, was to coach at college, and we were not at all surprised when Tommy Ellis, the head football coach at McMurry College, called and offered me a job in the summer of 1957. That job was as the head track coach and offensive line coach at McMurry.

Being the head track coach at McMurry gave me a tremendous amount of confidence and experience, both as a recruiter and as a person with the responsibility of running a college program. It also fit into our goal pattern: I planned to be an assistant coach in football for three years, and then move up to the head job in a small college. Yes, our goal was for me to become a head college coach in three years, and at the time I was just twenty-three!

Though my goal was to move up the ladder, Donell and I always had the attitude that we would bloom where we were planted, and every job we took, we would take as though it would be our last. That's a mental technique I've used to allow me to relax and do the best job I can do wherever I am, rather than always looking over the fence or worrying about where the next job is coming from.

True to my goals, before my twenty-sixth birthday I was named head football coach at McMurry. At the same time, I kept the head track job because I thought it would make me a more successful college football coach—and it did. I was able to recruit young men with speed who could participate in both sports.

My goal was now to be a head football coach in a small college for three years and then to move up as an assistant in a Division 1A school, which at that time meant one of the large universities. At the end of my third year, I had an offer from Southern Methodist University (SMU), but it coincided with McMurry's decision to drop scholarships. I did not believe that this policy was right, and so I stayed to change it. I worked with the board of trustees and the president, and finally convinced them to reinstate the scholarship program and to move McMurry up to a higher level of competition by joining the Lone Star Conference.

While going through the exercise of keeping scholarships at McMurry College, however, I turned down the opportunity to move into an assistant's position at SMU. My decision thus cost me a good position and another step up the ladder. It also cost me dearly in my record, because when they dropped the scholarships, McMurry lost a lot of key players who transferred to other schools. But it was very important to me to make sure that the job was finished, that McMurry was back on its feet as far as scholarships were concerned. It was important enough for me to know I had to turn down the SMU offer.

Three years later, in August of 1966, J. T. King of Texas Tech asked me to join him as the tight-end coach and recruiting coordinator. Donell and I decided to go. After three years at Tech, I was offered the head job at Angelo State University, which I accepted. Three years later, I was offered the head job at Baylor University, and accepted that, also.

Now my goals for Baylor moved into other three-year increments. The first was to build the football program. The second was to win the Southwest Conference championship. Sure enough, in my third year at Baylor, we won the first SWC championship in fifty years.

I served Baylor University for twenty-one years as head football coach, and even now, two years later, I have new, lofty goals I aspire to attain.

As a coach, teacher, motivational speaker, and father, I have found that teaching someone something they can use for a lifetime is very rewarding. During my career, I've been rewarded many times over by watching young men who seemed to be moving aimlessly through life all of a sudden understand the concept of goal-setting. To see their lives change, to know that nothing will ever be the same again for them, is a real thrill. This was exemplified by Aubrey Schulz, who came to Baylor from a junior college in East Texas.

Aubrey was an offensive lineman who could play defense, but he wasn't all that big, only about six feet tall and two hundred pounds soaking wet. The year Aubrey came to Baylor, I introduced him and all the other players to the concept of goal-setting. They looked at me strangely when I said that it was just as important to set goals academically as it was athletically. But they completed the goal sheets I had all ready for them to fill out in meticulous detail.

At the end of every school year, I had each player meet with his position coach, his academic coordinator, the trainer, and the strength coach, since all those areas were important to a player's total development. After the player finished talking to all the supervisors, he would set an appointment to come in and visit with me. I would take from thirty minutes to an hour with each player, talking to them about their goals, what they had achieved, and what they had to do in the future to achieve the goals they had set. If I felt that their goals were too high, I would ask them to carefully reset them, telling them that they had to realize that sometimes their desires were bigger than their capabilities.

When Aubrey Schulz came in at the end of his junior year, I looked at his goal card and reminded him that one of his goals was to be an all-American at Baylor University during his senior year. I said, "That time is not far away. Right now you're not even starting center on our team. You're not big enough, so how can you be an all-American?"

I never shall forget the look in Aubrey's eyes when he heard that. He looked coldly into my eyes, and said, "Coach, I am going to come back this fall and I'm going to weigh 230 pounds."

I said, "That's an awful lot of work and a lot of commitment."

He said, "I'm committed, and I'll do the work."

Aubrey Schulz came back that fall weighing 232 pounds, which is not very big according to today's standards, but was in 1974. He gained a starting berth on our team as an offensive center, and not only was all-Conference, but was a first-team all-American, helping lead his football team to the first championship at Baylor University in fifty years.

"I know having goals is important, so I try to get my freshmen to think in at least some general way about what they want to do," said Otis. "I tell them that I came from a poor background, too (since our county is rural and fairly poor) and I had a tough family life, and they cannot use that as an excuse. I tell them

'You are working for you, not your parents, nor Uncle Joe. You are working for yourself.'

"Then I go through a little exercise where I ask the kids to tell me what kind of lifestyle they think they want, and I write what they say on the board. Then I ask them how much they think it'll cost them. We go through how much their car payment will be, their house payment and utilities, food, and so on, and how much all that adds up to. Then I ask them what they're making in their part-time jobs now. Say it's $5.00 an hour, I tell them to make that $10.00, and yet when they add everything up, they find that even at $10.00 an hour they can't have the things they want. It wakes some of them up, because they think five bucks an hour is a big deal.

"I'd really like to find out what other teachers do to help their students become positive and goal-oriented."

Mike Singletary of the Chicago Bears—ten times Pro-Bowler—made the all-Rookie team his first year in the pros and has been all-Pro every year except one. Mike has not only been successful on the football field, but also very successful off, as a husband, a father, and a businessman. He has written a book and appeared on television, and is a motivational speaker and an inspiration to millions across this nation. Before all that, he played for the Baylor Bears.

So how did a frail, sickly little eighth grader get to be the great Mike Singletary?

The answer is—by setting goals.

Mike dreamed about playing football, getting an education, and becoming successful. But like so many, he was not equipped for the success he dreamed of. He was not always healthy as a child, and had a lot of problems to overcome. But he learned to set goals early. He wrote his goals down. He set goals in all areas of his life, and he stuck with those goals, allowing them to direct and guide his every action. He recognized that the attainment of every-day goals leads to the attainment of ultimate goals.

The first time I met Mike, I was recruiting him to come to Baylor University. I knew he was something special because, when I talked about academics, he listened and he asked questions. Although Mike had been a good player in high school, he did not receive the recognition that he would later receive at Baylor and in the pros. But I found him to be very intense and determined. He had all the characteristics that I call "intangibles." He had a very positive, strong-minded attitude, and he developed into one of the best goal-setters I've ever been around. His determination was unparalleled, and the power of his belief in himself and in a power greater than he, was truly outstanding. He also used the power of love in a very strong way. In fact, Mike taught me a lesson about love. I'll share that later.

To reach his goals, Mike Singletary had to overcome adversity. Using the power of the intangibles and the power of goal-setting, Mike Singletary has become one of the most successful individuals to ever play professional football. He received every honor he could receive, and is on his way to the Professional Hall of Fame. But Mike is more than that. He's a successful father and husband, a very successful business man, and one of the outstanding motivators of young people in the United States today.

The power of goal-setting.

> *"Not only we teachers, but also those of us who are parents, need to be reminded to help our kids realize that they can be whatever they want to be,"* said Sharon. *"And also that what they do today really affects what they can be tomorrow."*

4.
The Power of Determination

The intangible of determination is essential to success. Being determined keeps you from weakening when it becomes hard to maintain the daily effort you must make to reach your goals. Determination is the key to maintaining a positive attitude through all kinds of adversity. Determination allows us to overcome the bad things that happen. It allows us to keep that positive attitude even in the face of defeat, setbacks, and heartbreak. A determined person is one who will not quit.

I heard that sentiment one fateful day in Atlanta, Georgia. We were about to play Clemson University in the Peach Bowl, and CBS was televising the game. I had invited a former member of the Baylor team, Kyle Woods, and his family to attend the Peach Bowl, because Kyle had been a great inspiration to the Baylor team. The preceding August, Kyle had broken his neck during practice and become paralyzed from the neck down. He had spent many months in rehabilitation, trying to regain some movement in his hands and arms.

On the morning prior to the game, I asked Kyle to speak to the team.

The players had been motivated and moved by Kyle's courage and his sheer determination during the terrible pain and humiliation he had gone through after his accident. So they sat, breathlessly waiting to hear what Kyle would say to them that morning before the game.

Kyle realized that our team was a ten-point underdog to an outstanding Clemson team. When he spoke, he said to the team and the coaches, "I know how you got here. I know the heat of the Astroturf in Baylor Stadium [Floyd Casey Stadium] last August, and the trauma that you went through when I was injured. I also remember the tough loss to Alabama, and the great comeback against Texas Tech. And now you're here, playing on national television against a great team—Clemson University. I not only know how you got here, but I'm proud of what you've done to be in this Bowl.

"Now I want you to know how *I* got here.

"When I left Waco, I couldn't move anything except my mouth and my eyes. I went through some terrible times in Dallas as I went through rehab—and not only physical pain, but also psychological pain. But all the time there were two things that kept me strong, that kept me determined. The first was my faith. The power of belief cannot be underestimated. I believed then as I do now, with all my heart, that I had not been forsaken. I believed that some way, somehow, I would overcome the terrible things that were happening to my body, and I ultimately believed in myself as a person. That I had worth and value. That I could do something to make a contribution. The power of that belief sustains me to this day.

"The second thing that allows me to be with you today is what my grandmother taught me. Grandmother was eighty-seven years old when I was about ten. She took care of some of the children in my family, my cousins, my brothers and sisters. She had gnarled hands and walked on crutches. I didn't know it at the time, but now I understand that she had a severe case of arthritis. Every step she took, every sandwich she made, all the clothes she washed, caused her extreme pain. You could see it in her face.

"Grandmother recognized that I was worried about her. She called me to her side, sat me down by her big chair, leaned her crutches against the wall, and looked down at me. 'Kyle,' she said, 'I'm not going to lie to you and tell you that I'm not in pain. I know that you're worried about me and that you're concerned. I *am* in pain, but what I want to tell you is how I make it through every day, through the pain and through the heartache that the pain brings.'"

Continuing, Kyle said, "I couldn't wait to hear what my grandmother had to say. She looked at me with those loving eyes and said, '*I may give out, but I will never give in.*'"

After a dramatic pause, Kyle added, "That's it. The physical body is weak, but our spirit, our determination, is strong. If you won't ever quit, if you won't ever give up or give in, you can never be beaten." He smiled as he said, "Now the clock may run out with the other team ahead, but you're never beaten if you won't give in."

It was interesting to see what happened that day as we fell behind ten points in the fourth quarter and it looked as if Clemson was going to win. About midway through the fourth quarter, as the defense huddled, I saw them look to the sideline. There sat Kyle Woods in his wheelchair, wearing his Number 23 jersey and looking directly into the eyes of his teammates. That was the turning point. The defense not only held, but forced a punt. The offense rushed onto the field, drove the length of the field, and scored. We were now down only three points. Our defense held, and forced a turnover. The offense took over and scored, and we went ahead to win the game.

When the game was over, the team rushed over to Kyle Woods and picked him up, wheelchair and all, and paraded him around the field. Then they carried him over and let him accept the Peach Bowl trophy for the victory.

They had not given up. They had not given in. That had allowed them to find a way to win. All they could say to Kyle Woods was, "Thanks for teaching us the power of determination."

5.
The Power of Belief

There are literally hundreds of examples of the power of belief in an individual's life, but never has the collective power of belief been more evident than among Baylor's football team in 1974. In 1973, the team had been 2 and 9 in the won and lost column. At the beginning of the 1974 season, they lost their first two ball games to nationally ranked teams. Then they went on to win the SWC championship for the first time in fifty years!

Following the 1974 season, I wrote a book entitled *I Believe*. The title literally came from the seed that was planted my first day on the job at Baylor. Since Baylor had won three games and lost twenty-eight in the three previous years, many had recommended that Baylor just give up football and go on about its business. At my first press conference, I was asked the question, "Can Baylor compete and win?"

My answer was simple. "I believe that Baylor University can compete and can win, and at the same time build a program of integrity and respect, while developing and graduating student/athletes."

The fact that I believed it could be done carried over to my coaching staff, to the players, and ultimately, to those who supported the team. Of course, it began slowly. The first step I had to take was to surround myself with individuals who believed the job *could* be done. When I interviewed several members of the previous coaching staff, I was told, directly, that it was impossible to win at Baylor. They liked my attitude, they said, but in reality, the team could never win. Needless to say, those coaches never became a part of my staff! Those who did, believed that the job could be done.

A case in point was Bill Yung, a successful high-school coach who had played college ball at Texas Christian University (TCU). Bill called me several times after I arrived in Waco and started recruiting and building a staff. Finally we were able to talk on the phone, and he said, "I want to join your coaching staff."

Now I can tell you that there weren't a lot of folks kicking the door down to join a coaching staff that had such an awesome task ahead of them. But here was a guy who had a great job, was very successful, and yet wanted to be on my staff. So I asked him to meet me at four o'clock one afternoon in Waco.

That day I flew back in from a trip and walked into the office to meet Bill Yung. Bill was about 265 pounds, a former offensive lineman from TCU, a big guy—but I didn't stop to greet him on my way through the outer office. I just nodded to him to follow me. He came into the office. I walked around my desk and stood there behind it. He walked in front of my desk and stood there. I looked in his eyes. I leaned on the desk and said, "Okay you want to join our coaching staff. Why would someone who has a successful coaching job want to jump into a situation where most people say we cannot be successful?"

Bill leaned over, looked me right in the eye, and said, "Because I believe in *you*. And I believe that you're going to be successful, and I want to help you do it."

I hired the big fellow on the spot. He was

exactly what I was looking for: Someone who had talent, ability, and integrity, and who believed that the job could be done.

Belief, in a person or a program, cannot be falsified.

I knew I had to find bits and pieces in the program that I could begin to believe in. Then I had to exhibit that belief, and let others grasp it—particularly those individuals who needed someone to believe in them. Bill had been able to do that for me by believing in me. It meant a lot.

One individual from the 1972 team best represents all the young men who began to believe in themselves and to believe that Baylor could be successful on the athletic field. That one individual was Neal Jeffrey.

When I met Neal in the spring of 1972, he had been an unsuccessful freshman quarterback. He was a tall, lanky youngster, with a warm, engaging smile but a problem that was evident as soon as we began to talk. Neal Jeffrey was a stutterer, and as we talked, the conversation lasted a lot longer than I had expected it to, because it took Neal a long time to say what he wanted to say. Although I was impressed with the young man, I wondered how I could be successful with a quarterback who stuttered. But before we started spring practice, when I sat down and talked with Neal again, I told him his speech impediment was not going to be a problem with me, as long as he performed at the level I expected of him.

Neal did not possess great speed, but he was a hard worker, and had an excellent football mind. By the end of spring practice, he had beaten out all the other quarterbacks and was going to go into the 1972 season—as a sophomore—the starting quarterback for Baylor University. Because Neal believed in himself, in 1972 we surprised the football world by winning five football games and losing three others by less than three points. We were close to being 8 and 3, and going to a Bowl game. What a tremendous turnaround!

When the players were interviewed that year, they talked about their own personal confidence: the fact that they believed they could win, and they believed that they *would* win. But when 1973 came, the team's performance was detrimental to that deep belief. First of all, we played with a lot of brand-new players, freshmen we had recruited. They joined the older players on the squad and formed the nucleus of a team that later would be successful but which, in 1973, won only two games while losing nine. Many of the games were very close, and we lost because, with young players, we just didn't have the physical strength to win in the fourth quarter. That could be corrected. The important thing was that we kept growing closer because of the adversity the team faced.

The turnaround for the 1973 team, and for Neal Jeffrey personally, occurred in the homecoming game against TCU. The Southern Baptist Radio and Television Commission and the Fellowship of Christian Athletes had decided to create a series of 30-minute documentaries on ten individuals across the nation who were involved in some form of athletics. I was one of the ten chosen, and the film crews came the week of the TCU game. I envisioned this opportunity as a great recruiting tool for Baylor. Little did I know what was in store, not only for the team, but also for that film, which would be called *The Athletes—The Grant Teaff Story.*

During the game TCU jumped out ahead, and at half-time led 34 to 7. Then we made a dramatic comeback behind the arm of Neal Jeffrey. We were only six points behind, inside the ten-yard line with seconds to go, when Neal made a mistake. Thinking it was third down when it was really fourth, he rushed to the line of scrimmage, took the ball from the center, and threw it out of bounds to stop the clock. The crowd sat in stunned silence. You could hear my voice reverberating throughout the stadium, "No, Neal. It's fourth down!"

But the ball flew from his hand anyway.

As he realized what he had done, Neal came to me on the sideline, weeping openly. TCU ran the clock out and we trudged over to the dressing room. The cameras had been set up and the microphones were in place for a great celebration after a homecoming victory. But instead, they recorded a somber group in the dressing room. It hurts to lose a game. It hurts even more when you've come back, gotten close, and yet been unable to finish the job. It's even more painful when someone everyone respects is hurting as badly as was Neal. In his mind, it was his fault that we had lost the game. But in fact, had it not been for Neal, we would have lost badly. He had given us hope, he had given us inspiration, and had used his talent and ability to bring us close to the lip of the cup—the cup of victory.

What took place in that dressing room changed not only the lives of those in the room, but of thousands of others who have viewed the scene on film in the years since. Neal was seated to my left on the bench, head down between his legs, sobbing. We had our normal team prayer after the game, and I struggled for words to say to a team who had fought so hard but had still lost; a team whose players were still trying to believe in themselves and in the fact that Baylor could win.

I turned in Neal's direction and said, "Get your head up, Neal. You were the reason we had a chance to win that game."

In the background you could hear the voice of one of the players. "We love you, Neal."

And Neal's head came slowly up, tears drying on his cheeks. Every eye in the room was glued on him. Inaudible words moved his lips, forming the words, "Thank you." Those of us in the room did not realize it then, but that thank you was for the confidence the team was showing in him, with which we were able to regenerate the belief he had in himself.

The next year, even though the team lost its first two games, the players never swerved from their belief in themselves and the fact that they were going to win. The third game of the 1974 season was against Oklahoma State University. They were the eighth-ranked team in the nation when they came into Baylor Stadium, and they were playing a team that had lost 11 of its last 13 games. In spite of that, Oklahoma State was soundly defeated, and our team went on to perform in a miraculous way during the rest of the season, winning the SWC championship.

The key game in the 1974 season was again one in which Neal Jeffrey was the determining factor. This time however, the game had a positive finish. Baylor hadn't defeated the University of Texas in the preceding seventeen years. Texas had won six straight SWC championships and was well on its way to winning a seventh. Then, on a cool, rainy afternoon in Baylor Stadium, the history of the SWC was changed.

At half-time, Baylor was behind 24 to 7. Many Baylor fans began to file out of the stadium, some muttering, "Number eighteen down the drain." I don't know how many in the stands believed we could come back and win the game against the defending conference champions, but I don't think there were too many. As we walked back into the dressing room, I'm not even sure how many coaches and players for Baylor believed we could come from behind and win. But I know one young man who believed it, because I was walking up the tunnel with him. It was Neal Jeffrey. He turned and looked at me, put his hand on my shoulder and squeezed it a bit. A big smile creased his face. He was beaming with confidence as he said to me, "Coach, we're going to win this football game. I believe it with all my heart." That look of confidence on his face, knowing that we were down 24 to 7, filled me with an exhilaration that I have seldom felt in my whole life.

When we walked into the dressing room, Neal went

straight to the players and began to shake their hands and pat them on the back, and I heard him say, "We've got them right where we want them." By the time he had made it around the room, the atmosphere was electric. We had, in fact, established some things in the first half that were positive. We had moved the football, we had thrown the football successfully, and, though we were down 24 to 7 and Earl Campbell had made some yardage on us, we had played pretty decent defense. Yes, we had something to build on in the second half. But we needed something to turn the game around.

Texas was to receive the ball to start the second half. Our special teams, made up of individuals who normally did not start in the game, were filled with confidence because in the first half they had done everything they had been asked to do, and had done it successfully. Could they be the ones to turn it around in the second half?

Our defense held Texas. Texas's punt team came on the field, and the Baylor return team went on the field. But instead of lining up in the return, we put ten men on the line of scrimmage to block the kick. A crowd of Baylor players was on top of the punter before he could get the kick off. Johnny Greene jumped, extended his arms, and the ball struck his hands and bounced back toward the Texas goal line. Baylor recovered. Jubilation erupted on the sideline, and as Neal moved the offense to the field, I could see the smile on his face. We drove the ball down to the three-yard line, the score 24-7, the fourth down.

The slowest guy on either the offensive side of the field or the defensive side of the field was Neal Jeffrey. But I elected for him to keep the ball on a play action—run or pass. Neal ran to the corner of the field and stepped in just ahead of the Texas defender to score the touchdown. And, as they say, the rest is history. Baylor fought back, dominated Texas both offensively and defensively, and won the game 34-24! Baylor fans who had left the stadium and were listening on the radio in the fourth quarter, returned, leaving their cars on the street, and flooded into the stadium to be there when Baylor won the first game against the University of Texas in eighteen years.

Was it great coaching? No, it was good coaching, and a belief that was contagious. Neal Jeffrey, the leader of the team, believed that we could win, and his belief was infectious, and an entire team and the Baylor people began to believe.

Ah, the power of belief! It's not only important to believe in yourself and what you are doing, but you can give a great gift to others by believing in them, by displaying confidence in them as individuals and in their ability. One of the reasons I wanted to coach and teach was that my high-school coaches had instilled in me the confidence that literally changed my life. They believed in me as a person, and as a football player. They believed that I was of worth and value, and that I *could* be successful. As a teacher I had the opportunity to return to my students that which others had given me, to be able to put my hand on the shoulder of a young man, look him in the eye, and say, "I believe you can do the job."

On one occasion in particular my belief in someone won another SWC championship for Baylor. In 1980, we were undefeated. We were playing SMU, which had a very good football team. In fact, it was so good that at half-time they were ahead by 21 points. And what a football team establishes in the third quarter, whether behind or ahead, in most cases goes on to determine if they're going to win or lose the game. Our objective in the third quarter was to take the opening kickoff, drive it the length of the field, and get ourselves back in the game. But that didn't happen. Instead, at the Baylor eighteen-yard line, our quarterback—Jay Jeffrey, Neal's brother—sprinted to his left, turned to throw the ball back across the field to our wide receiver, and in so doing, threw it directly to an SMU defensive back. His name was Simmons, and he was an all-American, and he didn't have to do a great deal of running. He just sort of walked into the end zone. His team kicked the extra point, and the score was 28-0 early in the third quarter.

When SMU scored, I'm sure Jay Jeffrey thought about going off on the other side of the field, but he had to come off on our side. He really didn't want to face me, and tried to hide himself behind other players on the sideline. But I caught his eye and motioned for him to come to me.

As soon as he reached me, he looked me in the eye and said, "Am I going to get to go back in the game?"

Now that was a perfectly sound question, because here was a young man who had just thrown an interception that had put his team—an undefeated team, I might add—in jeopardy of losing a game, down 28-0. But when Jay asked me the question, I reached out and put my right hand on his left shoulder pad, folding his jersey up in my hand and pulling him close to my face so that he could hear what I had to say. His eyes were wide, probably anticipating that I was going to put him on the bench and choose another quarterback. Instead, I said, "Jay, I believe in you. You *are* my quarterback. I believe you can win this football game. Get back in the game and do it."

I'm not sure why I said what I said, with the exception of the fact that that really was all we could do. Jay had to rise to the occasion and I had to believe in him. He was the best we had, so why not say that?

I don't know how much that little speech on the sideline meant to him personally, but I do know that from that moment forward he was a different quarterback, and our team was a different team. Inspiring play from some led others to a higher level and allowed our team to come from behind and win, 34-28, to go on with an undefeated

SWC season, and to once again represent the SWC and Baylor University in the Cotton Bowl.

Would we have won that game without Jay Jeffrey? Would we have gone on and won our second championship? I believe the answer to both questions is no. I believe that the power of belief—my own belief—in that young man, instilled in him, and enabled him to instill in his team, the belief and desire and determination to come from behind and win.

The beautiful part about the story is that it is applicable to students on any day and in any area in which they are involved. As individuals, we are motivated by people believing in us. As teachers, we possess the power to believe in others.

> *"I believe that your students have to believe in you," said JoAnn, "and also that you must really believe in them. Then they'll open their minds up. They can tune you out very easily. At the first indication that you do not care, they can tune you out."*
>
> *"Last year I had a student who 'adopted' me as her mom," said Sharon. "She was often in trouble, but she brought me cards, called me 'Mama,' and she really loved me. She was very needy, and I found that the demands she made on me were very trying. But I stuck it out with her, and encouraged her, even though there were days when I thought I couldn't endure it another minute. Today that student is enrolled in a junior college where she is studying to be a child-care provider. She is the first in her family ever to graduate from high school, and the first to attend a college. I guess it all paid off. She needed encouragement. She needed me to believe in her. And I did.*

"But I realize that giving one child a great deal of attention can cause you to underserve the rest of the class, and you can't let that happen. Unfortunately, when you encounter a child who needs attention and affection desperately, it's really hard to deny them that, because it might be the only time he or she ever gets it."

6.
The Power of Caring

The Bible names three intangibles: faith, hope, and love. The Bible also clearly states that the greatest of these is love. There are certainly various kinds of love, and different degrees of love, and there are many different ways to express love. Love is the most powerful motivating force the world has ever known, and its dividend is caring. Very few people would give up their lives for a million dollars or some other material gain, but there are thousands of examples in history where individuals have willingly given up their lives because they cared. That deep caring may have been for an individual, a country, or for freedom. Whatever it was, the people who sacrificed were driven by the power of love.

Love fulfills you when you don't really expect it to, when you're doing something for someone else, or doing something just because you care. I played the game of football because I love the game. I dearly love the profession of coaching and teaching, and that love drives me to serve the profession.

Mike Singletary taught me something about love. When he was a junior at Baylor, he was one of our captains, and one day I had made a statement to the players that for us to become a unified team, we had to love each other, to care about each other. Mike stopped me after the meeting was over and said, "Coach, before I can love someone, I have to respect them."

What an astute observation. It is true: Respect is the stepping-stone to love. Love becomes a power in our lives, and caring is the dividend.

"I've been trying to teach the students to have more respect for themselves and one another, too," said JoAnn. "One of the ways I do this is to have a mirror in my classroom, up where the students can all see it. When someone starts to say something unkind or critical about someone, or to laugh at them rather than with them, I usually tell them to just look in the mirror before they continue that behavior. Eventually they begin to realize that their turn to be laughed at or to be on the receiving end of an unkind remark will come soon enough unless they change. I was greatly encouraged recently when someone said something unkind in my class, and the other students all told her to go look in the mirror.

"I also try to maintain close contact with my students. It's difficult, but I feel that someone has to care about them. I make a point of knowing my students' names within two days at the start of the year, and then I greet each one by name every day. I also give them a pat on the shoulder or a hug. It's amazing what you can do by touch. You never know what your students have come from before they come into your class, and somehow, somewhere, they need to know that someone cares.

"I started teaching before I had children of my own, and since I've had children of my own, I've had the attitude that I'm going to treat my students just as if they were my children. I'll discipline them when they need discipline and—strangely enough—they like that! They're not allowed to speak when I'm speaking, and that's a rule. I tell them, 'We're going to have some manners here.' And it works out well. We spend a lot of time away from subject material. We spend a lot of time on relationships. I tell them, 'You can't talk when he's talking. You're going to have to wait; you'll have your chance.' And you think, gosh, by the ninth grade, when they're fourteen years old, they'd know this. But they don't.

"I believe that if you can't set the tone of respect for each other, if you can't have discipline in your class, you cannot teach. I don't see how students can progress in classes where the teachers say, 'Oh, we don't have any rules. We just all do our own thing.' To me, you can't teach much in that environment. If you don't have discipline, you won't teach your students.

"Of course, you have to know when to bend the rules, too. It's interesting to go through your classes and listen to the students. Often, they'll complain, 'Well, my mother doesn't let me do (whatever),' and we'll talk about it and usually there's a good reason they weren't allowed to do whatever it was, and you ask then if they'd like to have a mother who would let them do anything, and they usually say no. They really want discipline. They want to know somebody cares."

"I agree," said Wally. "Being involved in

the Renaissance program has really changed the way I teach. I've had to relearn ways to relate to the kids, and I've had to find different ways to teach. I'm a lot more relaxed now, realizing that sometimes what the kids need more than anything is for a teacher to be involved with them and to care about them. I work at making my classroom nonthreatening. I don't relax my standards, but I respond to behavior differently. If the students cuss in class, I remind them that that's an inappropriate way to make a statement, but I don't go berserk. They don't need someone to condemn them. They need a gentle reminder of what appropriate behavior is.

"Recently, I had a kid who brought a gun to school. I spent the whole day down in the office with the student, and negotiated with the principal so that the student was only suspended for ten days. During that ten days I worked with his other teachers, and took work from their classes home to him. I felt that if I hadn't done that, I would've lost him, because all his brothers were in prison. I'm not saying I saved the kid, but I do think I had something to do with him staying in school. It sometimes takes that kind of effort. The kids have to find somebody they can attach to.

"I'm not saying that you can care that much about all of your students; but sometimes, if you see a slight indication that this one really wants to make good, that's what fires up your commitment."

In November 1992, I was about to coach my last regular-season game for Baylor University. It was against our arch-rival, the University of Texas, and it was to be played in Waco. There was a lot of excitement, and there'd been all kinds of television shows and newspaper articles talking about this being my last game. Our team was also excited about the possibility of winning, because if we beat the University of Texas, we had a chance to go to a bowl game.

It was a very emotional time for me and my family, because, having committed myself to the coaching profession at age thirteen, I had now reached the time when I would move from that beloved position to another. Everything seemed to be magnified for me, but in spite of that, I was able to keep the players focused on the fact that the game was significant because it was against the University of Texas, and not just my last game.

Prior to the game, we were out on the field for our normal warm-up procedures. I was standing about midway in the end zone when I felt someone beside me. I turned, and there stood a senior who had been given an extra year of eligibility because of an injury the year before. The senior was Trooper Taylor, from Cuero, Texas. Trooper's about five feet eight inches tall, and weighed about 175 pounds. He was a defensive back, one of the most personable young men I had ever coached, and a very dedicated football player. After his injury the preceding year, it had been mid-season before he'd been able to rehabilitate his knee and get back out for practice. By that time, others had taken his position as the return man, and as the nickel back on our defense.

As I turned and looked at Trooper, I saw tears in his eyes, and I immediately asked, "Trooper, are you okay?"

"No sir, I'm not," Trooper said.

"What's wrong?"

Trooper said, "I know this is your last game, Coach, but it's my last game, too. It's the end of my career here at Baylor, and I want to play in the game. I only lack breaking the school record on kickoff returns by eighteen yards. Will you let me return a kickoff for this game and play in the game?"

I said, "Trooper, it's important to me that you're going to get your degree and you've been working on your master's degree even this year. You've had a good career. You were unfortunately injured, and have not been able to regain your position on the team. Someone else now has the opportunity to play. It certainly was not your fault that you were injured, and it is not the fault of the young man who's taken your place."

He said, "But, Coach, do you understand how important it is for me to play? When I come back to Baylor Stadium and bring my family years from now, I want to be able to say to them that I played my last game as a senior, and I played in Coach Teaff's last game. It's very important to me. I'm not asking for a lot. Will you let me play?"

I said, "Trooper, the only thing I can tell you is I'll think about it."

When the warm-up was over, we were about to go into the dressing room for some last-minute instructions. Moving up the tunnel, I again felt a presence beside me and looked up. It was Trooper. He asked, "Coach, have you thought about it yet?"

I said, "Actually, Trooper, I have not, but I will."

There was a lot of excitement in the dressing room before we went back onto the field to play the University of Texas. When we were hurrying down the tunnel, I saw Trooper Taylor standing at the end of the tunnel, waiting for me. I walked by him, saying, "Trooper, I haven't had time to think about it. I'll think about it during the game."

We went onto the field and started the game. Texas kicked off to Baylor. We started to drive, and moved past midfield. Suddenly, following a thrown pass, I started to move to the north end of the coaching box. Just as I turned, I ran smack dab into none other than Trooper Taylor, who looked up at me and said, "Have you thought about it yet?"

I said, "Trooper, please move out of my way. I haven't thought about it. I will."

The first half went by quickly, and at half-time we were leading by a score of 14-7. As we went into the dressing room, I saw Trooper waiting by the door. I just shook my head as I went by. "No, Trooper, I haven't thought about it."

We went through the half-time procedures, and just as we were about to go out on the field for the second half, I saw Trooper waiting at the end of the tunnel for me. Scott Smith, the secondary coach who coached Trooper and the specialty teams, was standing about ten feet from me. I said, "Scott, come here a moment. This is Trooper's last game. He's a senior. He's done a great job for us. It's very important to him that he gets in the game. It's important to me that he gets in the game. I want him to return the kickoff because he only needs eighteen yards to break the school record."

Scott started to open his mouth to protest, because of all the preparation the other players had done, but I said, "No. Trooper's going to return the kickoff. And somewhere in the second half, put Trooper in the game so he can play."

We proceeded onto the field, and lo and behold, the ball was kicked to Trooper Taylor, who had a tremendous return, bringing it out forty yards and breaking the school record. He was jubilant, jumping up and down, bouncing off the field. Everyone was happy because Trooper's return gave us great field position and we were able to go on and score, moving ahead 21-7.

Texas came back in the third and fourth quarters, and came to within one point of our score. With two minutes to go on the clock, the score was 21-20 in Baylor's favor. Texas was on Baylor's 38-yard line, fourth down and two. They were obviously going to go for the first down. All they really had to do was make one more first down, get a couple or three yards, kick a field goal, and win the game.

I was standing by the first-down marker when Texas came to the line of scrimmage. The quarterback took the ball, and on a deep handoff to the halfback, initiated a draw play. The halfback started toward the line of scrimmage. Baylor's defensive tackle slipped off his block and hit the ball carrier about two yards behind the line of scrimmage. The ball carrier started to fall forward, and as he did, it looked to me as if the trajectory of his flight would allow enough yardage for the first down.

As he was coming to the ground—and it seemed as if it were all in slow motion—from out of the right corner of my eye I saw a green flash. The ball carrier was hit in mid-air and dropped straight down! The player who made the hit jumped up and started leaping around, as did all the Baylor players on the sideline and field, because Texas did not make the first down and now all we had to do was run the clock out. J. J. Joe, our quarterback, rushed to my side for instructions. I told him, of course, to take the snap, drop to one knee, and let the clock run out.

"Texas," I said with a smile, "has no time-outs."

Then I saw a movement of green coming toward me from the sideline. It was the guy who'd made the tackle that had saved the game for Baylor. Jumping up and down was old Number Two—Trooper Taylor! You've never seen a broader smile or a happier young man, or a happier coach! Trooper Taylor had won the game by making an extraordinary play.

After the game was over, after all the jubilation and all the celebrating and all the excitement, I started up the ramp and saw Scott Smith. I asked, "Scott, why was Trooper Taylor in on the last play of the ball game?"

Scott said, "Coach, you told me to get him in the game, and I hadn't gotten him in, so I put him in."

I hugged Scott and said, "Thanks."

Trooper Taylor won the game for Baylor University. I don't know if another player could have done the same job. I just know that Trooper Taylor cared enough about playing in his last game to ask me repeatedly to allow him to do so. And I cared enough about him and his feelings to allow him to be in the game. And Scott cared enough about what I had asked him to do to make sure it happened. Three individuals, caring, produced the power to succeed.

Caring not only can produce the power to succeed, but it is a creator of high self-esteem, the last intangible I want to mention. If someone cares about you as an individual, you begin to take pride in yourself. And when you take pride in who you are and what you're all about, your self-esteem grows. Taking pride means that you really care; that it's important to you how you look, and speak, and dress; that it's important to you to be thought of as a winner. If you take great pride in yourself, in what you are doing, and in the people you are working with, your self-esteem will grow. Taking pride in positive qualities demonstrates that you care about yourself, and pride and caring create high self-esteem.

II.
Creating a Learning Environment

We control what goes into our minds by what we listen to, what we read or watch, and by those we associate with. To achieve excellence, we must put our minds under our control.

—Grant Teaff

INTRODUCTION
The Learning Process

It's obvious to me, as it is to many others, that the learning process works best in the proper climate or atmosphere. This means that the environment of a classroom or other site of learning must be conducive to the learning process. And I believe it's the teacher's mental approach that creates the climate or atmosphere, which then hinders or enhances the learning process.

It has been my experience that if a teacher requires a certain standard of behavior, that standard will translate into a mental approach that everyone in the class will adapt to. We all know that the reputation of a teacher precedes that teacher; students pass on to other students what they have experienced in his or her class. This helps set the learning environment. For instance, if a teacher's approach is to allow challenging discussion, and his or her reputation with other students bears this out, the climate for thinking and challenging is created and the students come into the classroom expecting that type of environment.

7.
Discipline

For any structure to be long-lasting, for learning to reach full potential, and for success to prevail in the classroom, it has to be built on a strong, solid, sound foundation. I believe discipline is the best foundation on which we can build. I believe that personal discipline must be taught to and mastered by the students, since disciplined students help create a disciplined classroom.

Students are quick to recognize a teacher's personal discipline or lack of it. It's no longer good enough to simply say, "Do as I tell you." Now it must be, "Do as I say for these reasons, and because I have found success by doing it as well." The idea of discipline must be nurtured with evidences of success and underlined with respect for everyone, since respect is the key to discipline as well as to love.

I believe that to establish discipline, it's important to lay out the ground rules for the students, and these ground rules should cover behavior and conduct in the class, as well as the teacher's expectations of his or her students. Then I think it's imperative to stick to those ground rules, at the same time being firm but fair. What are reasonable expectations? I always told my incoming freshmen, "When I am speaking, I expect you to listen to me. I've worked hard to prepare to teach. I've worked hard so I can benefit you and help you make progress in learning and ultimately to succeeding in your own life. Therefore it's important to listen to what I say. How can I tell when you're listening? By your concentration. It is, of course, possible to appear to be listening and not hear a word someone is saying. Listening is a personal choice. But I expect you to sit up straight in your chair and listen. Sitting up in your chair has a tendency to keep you awake and alert, and it shows respect. When I'm speaking, not only you will not speak, but you will listen. In turn, when you are speaking, I will not speak, and I will listen."

Strangely enough, my own personal self-discipline once caused me a little problem. In December of 1992, I coached my last football game for Baylor University. So in 1993, a television network asked me to be the color analyst for Southwest Conference football. I knew I had the expertise, but I was not sure about all the technical aspects of the actual production of a televised football game. Nevertheless, I agreed.

When I started, I found out that in the announcer's booth you have three television monitors to watch, plus the play on the field. I had a play-by-play announcer to my right, a production assistant in the booth, and a camera man. I wore a headset with a microphone on it so I could talk and be talked to without anyone hearing it over the airwaves. I had a tremendous problem with this because of my firm belief that when others talk, I should listen. I would be describing a play, and the producer would give me some information about a playback or an upcoming commercial, so I would stop in mid-sentence and listen to what he had to say. Obviously, my strong belief was working against me. So I had to use personal discipline to overcome the habit I had developed over a long period of time. I had to learn that it happens to be okay to talk when someone else is talking—if you're live on television.

My emphasis on teaching self-discipline to my freshman class—particularly on listening and not talking when someone else is talking—caused me a slight problem on another occasion. It was in a Sunday School class I was teaching. I had a diversified age group that morning, and in the class was one young man of about twenty-eight who had a reputation for interrupting the teacher. I had just started teaching when I looked up to see one of my freshman football players walk in with his sister and sit down in the back of the room. The interrupter immediately began to interrupt. I was mid-sentence when he interrupted on two occasions with a question or comment. Each time, I courteously said to him, "I'll get back to that. Let me finish my point."

The third time the young man interrupted, I could see the freshman football player out of the corner of my eye. He was a 285-pound guard, and I saw him beginning to rise from his seat, glaring at the young man who had been interrupting. I caught his eyes with mine, and somehow indicated that he should sit back down, which he did. After we'd finished the class, the freshman approached me with wide eyes and said, "Coach, doesn't that guy know that nobody talks when you're talking? If you hadn't looked at me when you did I was thinking about putting his lights out."

Fortunately nothing of that nature happened. But the point was very clear. The freshman had adapted properly to the environment I had wanted to create as a learning climate for our football team. He *knew* no one should speak when I was speaking. In his mind, the ground rules had been established.

> *"If you don't have discipline in your class," said David, "it makes the kids very uncomfortable. When the year starts, if I have a*

freshman or sophomore class I often spend a couple of days laying the ground rules for the class, telling them what my expectations are of their behavior. I also spend time doing team-building activities. We'll go outside and do something as simple as playing Mail Call. This is a game in which we get into a circle and take turns as the one in the middle. I'll start in the middle and ask everyone who is wearing boots to move around the circle, and whoever is not wearing boots gets to go into the center and call out another specification, like all those wearing earrings, and so it goes on until everyone's been in the center once. It just kind of relaxes the kids and helps break down some of the barriers. We'll also do blindfold activities to build up trust. Students take turns blindfolding one another, and a seeing person is paired with one who is blindfolded. Then I'll give them a task— like taking make-believe plutonium from one side of the room to the other—and the seeing student has to guide the blindfolded student. It builds up trust and team effort."

"I do similar team-building activities," said Wally. "I have the kids write down one thing about themselves that no one else in the class knows, and then they hand the paper to me and I read it out. The other kids then try and guess who it refers to. They really like doing this, and it's a great way to get them to relax.

"I start off the year by trying to teach the kids respect. I don't like the word 'discipline,' so I tell the kids that I'm going to outline some procedures that will help us get along. For instance, I won't talk when they're talking. I *will listen to them. I will respect them. But I expect them to do the same to me. I don't expect them to talk when I'm talking, and I do expect them to listen to me. I try and explain that I'm not there to try and apply rules to them, but that unless there is mutual respect, we won't be able to get anything done.*

"I'm really big on trying to teach them self-discipline. I've got twenty to thirty kids in my classes, and there's no way I can watch all of them all the time. So there has to be a certain amount of self-discipline, respect, and trust. I tell them that I've got to be able to believe that they're going to do what they're supposed to do. Then I spell out the consequences they will incur for every bad action they take. I think this is something that the kids in ninth grade often don't understand. They think they can blame their behavior on something that happened at home or in another class, but I try to teach them exactly what will happen if they choose badly. With the at-risk kids, this is particularly important. I have to tell them exactly what will happen if they bring a gun or a knife to school, and I have to make it stick.

"To hammer home the point, I take the newspaper and we go through it talking about what happened overnight or at the weekend. So if there's been a gang fight, or if someone got stabbed, we then talk about what the consequences will be for all those involved. I can say to them, 'Well, I know you guys are Eastsiders, so I know you know who was involved in this fight. But do you know why it happened? Is there some other way that situation could have

*been resolved?' They know that when they tell
me something confidential, it'll stay with me,
unless someone is at risk. And so the kids begin
to trust me. Respect, trust, and learning the
consequences of their actions have a real effect
on these kids.*

*"I'm part of a three-teacher team that
does this, and the other teachers are very
supportive. We have 1800 kids in our school,
and we often think of the beginning of the TV
show Dragnet, where they used to say something like, 'There are a million stories out there,
and this is just one of them.' Well, we have
1800 kids, and they're coming to school every
day, and some of them didn't eat breakfast,
and some of them were beaten up by Dad last
night, and some of them didn't even go home
last night—we'll probably never know all their
stories. There's some kids we'll never reach, but
I guess it's the ones that show some signs that
they do want help that we are able to touch."*

*"My students learn the consequences,
too," JoAnn said. "I've found that my height
(JoAnn's about 5'8") helps tremendously. I had
a student who was standing behind me recently, and he said, 'If you don't turn around,
I'm going to stab you.' And I said, 'No, you're
not. You're going to come with me.' He was
smaller than me and I really could have de-
fended myself against him. And I knew this
student. I knew he didn't have anything to stab
me with. He was just bluffing. He wanted
attention.*

*"As well as getting to know all 140 of my
students' first names in the first two days, I've
found something else that really works. I give*

my students Christmas cards every year. I put their names on their cards and then put them on the bulletin board. They are so thrilled with them. I don't know how many students have told me that the card I gave them was the first Christmas card they had ever received. They just don't get Christmas cards. I also give them candy for Valentine's, and Valentine cards. Every month when there's something special, I do my bulletin board to highlight that. Next month is St. Patrick's Day, and I'll do something green, and I'll give the kids candy. Candy's against the rules, but sometimes you have to bend the rules. I just think the kids need something really special that helps them identify with you. They love you. You love them.

"When I was at school, I had a first-grade teacher who absolutely ignored me. I was from a very poor family, and I was this little kid in poor clothing and cotton socks, and I was totally non-existent to that teacher. I would put my hand up to read, and she would ignore me. If I had to go to the bathroom, she would ignore me. It was a terrible year for me, and to this day I remember that teacher. I knew she did not care about me, and she is with me every day in my mind. I can't remember one thing she taught me, but I knew when I became a teacher that I did not want to be like her. It has really influenced me to make sure the kids know I care.

"One thing I have to add is that when you're a football coach in college, you get to choose your students. We don't have a choice. We are given twenty-five or twenty-eight students, and we just have to do what we can with

them. I live in a very poor economic area. We lack a lot. But if the students can see caring in me, if they know they are loved, hopefully it will be reciprocated.

"I have very little trouble with my students, and if they come into my classroom looking troubled or sad or something, I make them go back to the door and practice coming in with a smile. I act silly a lot. I'm really crazy. I try to build up a sense of humor, and help the kids to learn to laugh at themselves. Humor works."

"I agree," said Sharon. "I encourage my students to laugh with me if things go wrong in the classroom. The kids really pick up on your mood, whether you mean for them to or not. I've had kids to come into my class and say to me, 'Smile!' And I'll realize that I was still reacting to the class I'd just had, and I didn't even know I was. Then I realize that I can't make this class pay for what I've just gone through in the last class, and I change my attitude. So our students really do influence our lives, too.

"Also, I think when you've been at a school a long time, the students know you're going to be there and they come back and visit you, bring their babies, sometimes years after you've taught them. I think it's critical that a teacher knows her students on an individual basis and cares about them. That's what the students really need."

"The sad thing is that I know teachers who don't want their students to get close to them. They believe in just lecturing to their students all day, day after day. They don't want that closeness," said JoAnn.

"But there's also a lot of teachers who really care and yet who get burned out. Some start out really caring, but the effort and the involvement that good teaching takes today just wears them out," said David. "I have an Algebra I class made up of seniors. Now Algebra I is usually taken in the freshman year, so these students are those who have struggled to get this far and still need to pass the Algebra I course to be able to graduate. Some of them were really getting stressed out, so I called a mandatory meeting for the class and their parents at a local restaurant one evening, where I told them I would treat them to tea or cokes. My idea was to take some of the stress off them. Of the nine students in that class, seven showed up with their parents.

"We just talked and socialized for about an hour. Then I talked about graduation and told them how great it was that they would be graduating. Most of them would be the first in their families to do so, and they had a lot of questions about it. Some of them had been absent from the Algebra I class quite frequently and were ready to quit, so I spent a lot of time encouraging them, telling them that they needed to work just a little harder and they would be able to graduate. One of the students came to me two weeks after that meeting and said that he had been going to drop out, but now he was going to try and stick it out and pass Algebra I and graduate.

"I like interacting with my students like that, but it does wear you out."

As a student, I learned from first-hand experience that the lack of discipline in a classroom can cause chaos, and in one instance, an embarrassing situation for me. As a sophomore in high school, I behaved in a less than acceptable manner. Later, when I thought about it, I realized my conduct was poor and I was embarrassed by it. But I believe it was poor because I sensed there was no discipline in the classroom. I was not alone in this. The other students in the class obviously sensed the same thing, because their behavior was like mine—terrible!

On the first day of school that sophomore year, I walked into a math class. The teacher was hesitant, seemingly unsure of himself, and established no pattern of discipline. From the first day, people were talking in the class, being disruptive and disrespectful. I knew better, because from day one in my personal life I had been taught the importance of self-discipline and respect for others, the importance of saying "Yes, sir," and "No, sir," and "Yes, ma'am" and "No, ma'am," listening when talked to, and all the basic disciplines that give us the opportunity to achieve success. But, even though I knew better, I did not behave as I had been taught, but rather joined in the disruptive behavior of the others.

Interestingly enough, not only did we disrupt the opportunity of others in that class to learn, but our behavior was detrimental to me personally. The foundation in math that I needed to attain that year went by the wayside because of my lack of discipline and respect for the teacher. The very next year I flunked the math course, and that failure almost sent me to an early career as a private in the U.S. Army.

I'm very ashamed of my behavior in that sophomore math class, and I hope that if that particular math teacher reads this, he will accept my profound apology.

Because of this and other incidents, I believe strongly in the need for discipline, particularly self-discipline, and in that, I'm in distinguished company. Nolan Richardson, the head basketball coach for the University of Arkansas, not only is one of the outstanding basketball coaches in America, but is also a firm believer in discipline. In an article in *USA Today*, Richardson talked about discipline in his own life, and the importance of discipline in the success that his teams have had over the years. It was 1958 when Richardson came face to face with one aspect of discipline. He was playing football at Bowie High School in El Paso, Texas. After his coach, Lou Robustelli, received his students' grades, a trip to the coach's office was inevitable for Richardson, since he had failed one of his five classes. In his office, Coach Robustelli was waiting with the paddle. Five swats was all that it took, and Nolan Richardson never failed another class.

Of course, nowadays, the paddle is a relic of the past, and Nolan Richardson, like others, is concerned that a sense of discipline has been eroded as a result of its demise. In the *USA Today* article, Richardson, now 52 years old, was quoted as saying, "You'd be surprised at how that board became a source of motivation. When that was taken away, there were guys flunking right and left because the discipline had left."

Richardson recognizes that these are different times, and says, "Today, if you look at kids sideways, your life is in jeopardy. It's crazy. So I tell kids the most important thing is self-discipline. If we can't get [discipline] through some other place, then you've got to try to discipline yourself." On the basketball court, Richardson teaches a philosophy of a disciplined attack with great self-control.

Nolan Richardson's mother died when he was three, his father when he was twelve. He was raised by a grand-mother who taught him the value of common sense, and, of course, discipline. And as an African-American growing up in the South, Richardson has faced his share of adversity, so the self-discipline he developed because of his grandmother and others has been vital. He's been able to rise above all that adversity and find personal and professional success. His record at the University of Arkansas—205 victories and 74 losses in nine seasons, with six consecutive NCAA tournament bids—is not only remarkable, but one of the best in the history of the game. In 1994, Coach Richardson's Razorbacks won the National Championship.

Nolan Richardson's life was changed by a high-school coach who cared enough to visit on him the consequences of his actions. Today we might have to use different methods, but creating an environment of discipline in our classes very well may allow a youngster the first glimpse of discipline in his life.

When I read the story about Nolan Richardson being paddled by his high-school coach, I was reminded of two experiences that dramatically shaped my life. The first occurred when I was about two years old and living in the small town of Hermeleigh, Texas. My father was working at a local gin at the time, while I was entering the "terrible twos" phase of my life. Evidently something didn't go exactly the way I wanted it to go one day, so I had a temper tantrum. While I was lying on the floor, screaming, kicking, and flailing my arms about, my dad walked in the door. I can say without hesitation that that was the last temper tantrum I've ever had while not being in control. (I've had one or two on the sideline when an officiating call was adversely affecting my team, but I must admit that most of that was show, and I was completely in control.) I don't remember if my dad used his hand, or his belt, or maybe a paddle he had stored away for such an occasion, but I do know he never had to administer corporal punishment to me again. That was the first and the last spanking I received from my dad.

The second experience came a little later, when I was in high school. At that time, I thought playing high-school football was the most important thing I could be doing with my life, since I wanted to coach. But I found out that there was more to achieving success than just what I did on the football field.

For several weeks I had taken Friday mornings off from school, and had been undetected. Arriving at school on Friday mornings, I would walk down the hall, leave out the back door, and go a few blocks down to a place on Deep Creek that provided a good place to lie in the shade of a big cottonwood tree. For lunch I would walk about a half-block to a little cafe on the other side of the tracks. I would have stew with my friends there, and talk about the ball game coming up that evening. At five o'clock promptly, I would walk into the little field house—actually a barrack that had been converted to a locker room—located at the south end of the stadium.

All had gone well until one fateful day prior to the Colorado City game. That evening, when I opened the door and walked in, my high-school line coach, Mule Kizer, was standing in the middle of the room, his arms folded. Stacked neatly in front of him, forming a pile about a foot and a half high, were pieces of kindling wood. Every eye in that locker room was turned on me as I walked in.

Coach Kizer asked, "Where have you been?"

I would never have considered lying to Coach Kizer, so I told him, "Coach, I've been down Deep Creek, resting. I had lunch with my friends across the tracks, and I feel I am mentally ready to play the game tonight."

In front of everyone, Coach Kizer said, "It takes more than discipline on the football field to be successful. You have to learn discipline off the field. It's just as important for you to be in class on time as it is to be here, at a meeting, on time. Now, bend over."

Humiliated, I bent over in front of my teammates, and Coach Kizer started with the kindling at the top of that pile of wood and worked his way all the way to the floor. My

73

teammates were ducking and dodging the splinters and pieces of the board as they ricocheted off my lower half. Still, I don't remember the pain as much as I do the humiliation and, even worse, the fact that I had disappointed and upset my coach. Like Nolan Richardson, I learned my lesson. I never missed another class. Being prompt and being where I was supposed to be became important parts of my own personal self-discipline, and, I believe, should be to all those who want to be disciplined individuals.

Of course, setting an environment of discipline requires more than punishment for not doing what you're supposed to do, but it *is* one important element of it. Students have to understand that there are negative consequences for negative actions.

> *"It's hard to help students realize the necessity of self-discipline, especially when a lot of the parents in our county did not have a great deal of education themselves, and they don't place a high priority on it. They don't really care about it," said Otis. "I've had some parents, even those with higher education, tell me not to give their children homework because that's what school is for. The attitude is, 'You take care of this in school. I've got things for them to do at home.' Lots of parents say this. It's been a real eye-opener for me."*
>
> *"You have to get the kids enthused," said Cindy. "I heard about one teacher who held an academic pep rally before her students had to take a state test. They had a motivational speaker come in and one of the athletic coaches gave a pep talk, just as he would for a sports pep rally. The teacher said it was great; the students were in a relaxed and confident*

frame of mind when they took the exam. I thought it was a great idea."

"We have a nationwide program called VICA—the Vocational Industrial Arts Club of America [See Appendix]," said Doug Webster, of Charlotte, Vermont. "I'm state director for the competition that VICA sponsors, and it takes an approach that is similar to athletic programs. It's a hands-on program that encourages competition in automotive skills, leadership skills, job interview skills, and other work-place skills."

"The FHA [See Appendix] has something like that, too," said Cindy. "In their competition they have to show what skills they've learned in their vocational home economics classes. So there are programs to encourage skills out there. I guess we just have to work harder to make academics count."

8.
Creating a Mind-Set

Creating the right learning environment also helps create the proper mind-set, and in turn, a proper mind-set helps create the right learning environment. It's the old question: which comes first, the chicken or the egg? I believe the teacher's attitude is like a single candle, which, when lit, can light one candle at a time until there is a blazing light in the room. The attitude of the class must be set initially by the teacher.

As a teacher, I am aware of the importance of communication. I use my ability to communicate every day. I know that I communicate with my body language, sometimes even unknowingly. I'm aware that I communicate with my expressions and particularly with my eyes. And, of course, vocal communication was an essential part of the education process for all those in my football program.

Many student/athletes came into our football program at Baylor with absolutely no communication skills. To address this problem, at the beginning of every season, I laid the foundation for success with each incoming freshman class, holding a three-day seminar on leadership and personal development. Although it was not an academic class, the atmosphere I created was exactly the same as I would have created had it been an academic class. At the outset, I gave the class an overview of what we would accomplish in the three days we would be together.

After the overview, I wrote the following list of objectives on the board:

1. Getting to know each other.
2. Developing unity.
3. Developing communication skills.
4. Knowing and understanding how the college system works.
5. Recognizing in yourselves the capacity to succeed.
6. Recognizing leadership capabilities in yourselves and others.

I told them that we would place great emphasis on self-motivation, goal-setting, self-discipline, and communication. I then set the guidelines to be followed during our time together. These included sitting up straight, concentrating on what I had to say, and opening their minds to receive information that would help them become successful students, graduate from Baylor University, and ultimately become useful citizens able to contribute to their community.

I stressed the importance of self-discipline. I asked them to follow in the classrooms on campus the guidelines I set in my own classroom. This meant treating their professors and other teachers with respect. Teachers work hard to prepare to teach, I told them, and disrespect for that preparation in the form of not paying attention or of not giving the proper effort could have a very negative effect on the teachers.

Next, I told them what would be happening in the weeks ahead, based on my experience. Some of them would become homesick and even want to go home, I said. Others would become discouraged on the football field. They would have to deal with this reality: If you want to succeed, you have to be willing to compete for your goals.

Following the reality check, I would teach them how to set goals, then how to evaluate their own intangibles. Then we would begin the process of learning to communicate by actually communicating. To start this, at the end of each class session I would divide the class into groups consisting of five or six students. I would appoint one of the players in the group to be the leader, and his responsibility was to carry through with the goal of the group. This was to learn all about each other as quickly as possible, and in so doing, to reach a comfort zone with their teammates.

To accomplish this, each member of the group had to stand and relate to the other members of the group his full name, anything unusual about himself, the football position he played, and his major goal. When he left class that day, each student had to know the full name, position, and goal of all the members of his group, as well as something unusual about them. At the next class meeting, I would randomly call on individuals to name the members of their group. The groups would change so that there were at least four members new to each group every day. At the end of the first three days, all of the students would know each other and know something unusual about each other.

The forced "getting-to-know-you" experience had two benefits: improving communication skills, and generating a sense of belonging.

This last was particularly helpful with Steve Renaldo, who came to Baylor from the state of Colorado. When I recruited Steve, I knew that he was hearing-impaired, and his ability to speak had been hampered by that physical problem. I was concerned about Steve, so when I broke the class into small groups, I positioned myself close to the group of which he was a member. In his group were a quarterback, two running backs, and a fullback. Steve was the last to talk about himself, and he said, "The unusual thing about me is that I talk a little differently than others because I'm hearing-impaired. But you won't be able to tell that when I tackle you in practice." That broke through the discomfort that the other players might have been feeling, and Steve immediately became a vital part of the freshman class.

Accountability

With the freshmen, I spent time emphasizing the control each of us has over our own mind. First, I told them, we control what goes into our mind by what we listen to, what we read or watch, and, interestingly enough, by those we associate with or talk to. Since our mind controls our actions and our emotions, the sooner students learn this one fact, the sooner they can be held accountable for their own behavior. Such adages as "Think before you speak," "Look before you leap," and "Mind over matter. If you don't mind, it doesn't matter," are keys to reinforcing this.

I reminded the players that, to pursue and achieve excellence in any endeavor, they had to harness the power of their minds and put it under their control. That put the responsibility squarely on their shoulders. Therefore, their conduct in class and their behavior patterns on and off the football field belonged to them, and they had to remind themselves continually of their responsibility to "take care of business." (This theme of taking care of business is addressed at greater length later in the book.)

Athletes have a tendency to be supercharged with emotion. Since most sports are played better with emotion, it is imperative that athletes learn to *control* their emotions. People in control of their emotions are less likely to do something they will be sorry for, to say something they'll be sorry for, or to participate in an action they'll later regret. We live in a society and a time when young people are settling arguments and confrontations with violence, so it is vital that all of us, parents, educators, and other adults, teach the importance of self-control.

Control

Control wins football games, and that can be readily demonstrated. In 1992, Baylor University was playing TCU, and it was an emotional game. During the game, the Bears received seven 15-yard penalties. Normally, a team couldn't win a game under such a burden. However, we did win, and the situation with the penalties gave me a great opportunity to teach. The day after the ball game, I spent more than an hour with the team, pointing out that each 15-yard penalty could have been avoided. Instead of putting ourselves in a position where we had had to fight down to the wire and barely win the game, we could have comfortably coasted in the fourth quarter if we had not made those critical errors of control.

For example, when you tackle the quarterback after he's thrown the ball, you automatically get a 15-yard penalty. This is because the defensive player rushing the passer knows when he's thrown the ball. The pass rusher should immediately stop his momentum, or direct it away from the quarterback. He should never hit the quarterback after he's thrown the ball! During the TCU game, we hit the quarterback late three times! All three times TCU would have had to punt the ball, but instead we gave them a first down by not being in control.

On two occasions, our players were pushed after the play was over. Acting like little banty roosters, they turned around and pushed back, knowing that the second individual in such a situation will always get caught. The flags will fly, and another 15-yard penalty will be logged. Sometimes, if the push is flagrant enough, it could even result in expulsion from the game, another major penalty.

In addition to these incidents, during the TCU game we also had two pass-interference calls, for which there is just no excuse. Defensive backs are taught the proper techniques for breaking on the ball, and how to intercept or knock the ball down without touching their opponent. But on two occasions we had touched the opponent and gotten two more 15-yard penalties.

We had to do something before the next week's game, which would be against an excellent football team that liked to intimidate its opponents. So our plan for the game was simple: We would incur no 15-yard penalties, and would have complete control of our emotions. By consciously controlling our emotions and actions, we immediately would make ourselves a better football team with a greater chance to be successful. If someone pushed us from behind or said something out of line, we would merely turn, smile, look at them and walk away, creating frustration in the individual who was trying to intimidate.

With this in mind, the players went into the game feeling that they had something over their opponents. That something was control, and a plan. On two occasions during the game, I was looking directly at one of our players when he was pushed from behind. He stopped, turned, and smiled at his opponent, who immediately became frustrated, and, on one occasion, even got a penalty himself. Our players were confident because they knew that their teammates were not going to get a foolish 15-yard penalty. All great plays would stand because there would be no 15-yard penalties.

In fact, there were none during the remainder of the 1992 season. A great tribute to control.

Making Chicken Salad out of Chicken Feathers

When I was playing football in high school, I quickly learned that I had to find something within myself to offset my inadequacies. I was small and extremely slow. I had a good mind, but I knew it was going to take more. I decided that if I could know my opponent, I had a chance to defeat him one-on-one. And that's what football is all about. It's a team sport, but individual battles are going on in every play. Besides paying close attention to my coaches, practicing hard, and preparing myself mentally, I went two steps further. Those two steps changed my life and my coaching techniques.

Step One: I analyzed the film of our previous game. I would study myself for hours, finding faults in my own techniques that could be corrected. I knew that mastery of the individual techniques would make me a better player. It would not make me stronger, faster, or quicker, but I would have an advantage if I mastered my techniques.

I also analyzed my opponent, studying the player lined up in the position across from me. I looked carefully at his alignment prior to the snap of the ball. If he stepped with a certain foot, I knew that by stepping with the corresponding foot I could instantaneously offset the power he might have over me. By comparing the alignment of the opponent to the defensive play that was run, I could analyze the defense based on the guy lining up in front of me. It gave me a tremendous advantage, and made me look like a much better player than I was. I continued doing this through college and into my coaching career. Because we always analyzed the opponents' game film, many times we knew what play they were going to run when they came to the line of scrimmage. An offensive player might tip the direction of the play or whether it was a run or pass by the placement of his hands or feet.

While I was coaching at Angelo State, for example, our team was to play my old school, McMurry College. McMurry had a very strong running attack, and they used two set halfbacks in the backfield. When analyzing the film, we noticed that any time the ball was given on a straight hand-off to either one of the backs, that back would drop his left foot way back, so that a linebacker could see it on the field. So our middle linebacker was instructed to look for the McMurry back who dropped one foot behind the other. Then he was to call the signal, "Popcorn right," or "Popcorn left." That told the rest of the defensive players the direction of the play and the back who was going to get the ball. Needless to say, McMurry made very few yards on Angelo State that night. To this day, I'll bet you if either of those running backs hears someone yell "Popcorn," he'll run for cover. They were certainly covered up that night.

The essence of the plan is simple. Study your opponent. Know your opponent. Respect your opponent. Defeat your opponent. Whether the opponent is a player on the football field or a math course or a science project, the plan applies.

Step Two: I used a technique called visualization. This is the technique of seeing in your mind an experience, or in my case, an actual football game, played down by down, quarter by quarter. In his book, *Psychocybernetics*, Dr. Maxwell Maltz gives the reason this works so well: The subconscious mind can't determine the difference between what is real, and that which is vividly imagined.

My technique was to clear my mind, get in a quiet place, and play the entire ball game in my mind, going through all the different possible scenarios that could happen during a game. By the time the game arrived, I had already experienced it two or three times. On those Fridays when I would go down to Deep Creek before Mule Kizer put an end to that plan, (see the section on discipline) I wasn't just resting. I was visualizing the game that would take place that very night.

Practice has a tendency to make perfect, and you can practice in your own mind. It creates positive expectations and reinforcement, because you visualize yourself being successful. Great golfers, tennis players, and basketball players have said on numerous occasions that visualization has not only filled them with confidence and a positive outlook, but has given them the edge in competition.

"By the second day in my beginning drafting classes," said Don Bridgeman, of Flossmoor, Illinois, "I tell the students, 'Visualize this house. Now take a piece of paper and draw the way the house looks to you.' Of course everyone in the class draws something different, because they're seeing different things in their minds. Visualization is a key thing in all aspects of life, and that's what I tell the students. When you're working in your mind, visualizing, you always succeed. And when you confront the situation you have visualized, you're not scared because you know what to do.

"When I'm coaching, I tell the pitcher, 'Go home tonight. Visualize the game. Now you're coming to the last inning, the bases are loaded, their best hitter's up, and you are going to take him out. Visualize it, and you will strike him out. When that situation arises on the actual day of the game, you'll already have played it in your mind, and you'll know what to do. You'll know what pitch to throw, because you'll have already done it.'"

"I use visualization myself, and I find it very useful. I think that maybe I should try and have my students visualize success," said Wade Grove, of Oakland, Maryland. "With the students I'm dealing with, I need to encourage them to focus on the successes they do have, on

> *what they do have available. Maybe they could*
> *see a paper with a congratulatory message*
> *from me, like, 'Well done,' or something simi-*
> *lar, on it."*

All freshman coming into the football program at Baylor since 1976 have heard the following story, because it's a great example of successful visualization. It concerns the time Baylor flew to Auburn, Alabama, to play the University of Auburn. We had worked on visualizing a successful game against Auburn all during the week, but now it was almost game time. During the quiet time I spent with the players before the game, I told everyone that even if we played our best, it would be a close game. I said, "We have to expect to win, but more than that, we have to visualize the victory. It not only will fill us with positiveness as we go into the game, but it will let us know throughout the game, even when it is very close, that we will find a way to win."

Everyone in the room closed his eyes and relaxed as I painted a word picture for all of them to visualize.

"It's the fourth quarter, we're down by a touchdown and Auburn's driving on us. We're in a foreign stadium. A radical crowd is against us, and we're tired in the fourth quarter. Our backs are to the wall. They have first down inside our 5-yard line. Someone has to make the big play. We can't let them score. The only way we can keep them from scoring is to get the football. Someone is going to rise to the occasion and knock the ball loose. Who will it be? Who will recover the fumble? Now our offense finds its back to the wall. We're down one touchdown. We must drive the length of the field, score, and go for two points in order to win the football game. Who on offense will make the big play?"

I described a few of the plays I thought would be successful, then I moved the football down visually to the position inside the 5-yard line, at which point I said, "We take it in to score, seconds left on the clock. We go for two points with the play we've worked on, believing it will be successful against Auburn. We make the two points and win the football game!"

I felt an exhilaration as I described the game, and when we all opened our eyes, everyone was smiling and slapping each other on the back. We'd just won the ball game. However, we still had sixty minutes to play before this scenario could possibly come true.

Call it what you want—luck, a self-fulfilling prophecy, whatever—lo and behold, it all came true. In the fourth quarter we were down 14-7 against Auburn. They were in control of the game and driving for the cinching touchdown. Inside the 5-yard line, the Auburn tailback got the football just as our linebacker broke past the line of scrimmage and hit him head on. The ball squirted in the air. Our defensive end caught it in mid-air and fell on it at the Baylor 10-yard line. Everyone on the field for Baylor, and everyone on the sideline, knew that we were going to score. Why not? We'd done it a little over three hours earlier in the confines of our dressing room.

Some great plays were made by different individuals, and that kept the drive alive. We finally got inside their 5-yard line and scored. Now, a tie with Auburn after you've been down 14-7 might've been okay for some, but not for the fighting Baylor Bears. Victory was our goal. We successfully scored the two-point conversion, and won the football game 15-14! The feeling I experienced was without question one of the greatest I've ever had after a football game, because all the circumstances had come together to produce victory, and that football team had learned a lesson I doubt any of them has ever forgotten about the power of visualization.

Of course, visualizing yourself winning without having done the daily preparation just won't get the job done. But once the groundwork has been laid, visualizing simply allows you to learn and gain experience by simulating a situation in your mind. This can take place in the work place, in the classroom, or in the home. It works because you're thinking about your responsibilities and bringing clear focus to the task at hand.

During the period of time I spent each year with the freshmen in classroom surroundings, I developed an atmosphere for learning and success that permeated our whole football program. I laid the groundwork and planted the seeds, but for there to be a successful harvest at the end of four years, those seeds had to be nurtured, fertilized, watered, and cared for in a meticulous way. I wish I could say honestly that every freshman I spent those hours with thoroughly understood and responded positively to those things I tried to teach. However, we all know that's not the case. Sometimes it was years before they really understood what I was trying to do and what I was trying to teach. Then I would get a telephone call or a letter saying, "Coach, I finally understand what you were talking about."

After all, teaching is like casting out the seeds of opportunity. The end results depend on where the seeds land, and it's very difficult to grow anything on a rock. But sometimes in a creative, disciplined learning atmosphere, rocks can be turned into fertile soil, and success beyond everyone's imagination can be reached.

9.
Effort and Errors

Effort

I believe that nothing can replace trying or giving of our best. When I was a small child, I would go to the cotton fields with members of my family. When the cotton was ready to pick, everybody had to pitch in and harvest it. Everyone was paid according to the amount of cotton he or she picked, and this provided me with an economic lesson: *The more effort you give, the greater your reward.* Thus I believe that giving effort and expecting effort sets the proper tempo in a classroom.

As a child in the cotton fields, I learned that it wasn't how quickly you proceeded down the rows of cotton that counted, or the weight of the cotton sack, it was the quality of the bolls that you picked. Mature cotton weighs less than a green boll, and for a child, the temptation was to put in a few more green bolls so they would weigh more. But once the cotton sack was emptied and the green bolls were revealed, not only did you lose credibility, but you lost the value of the sack of cotton.

Bending over all day and pulling a cotton sack behind you is back-breaking work, and it enabled me to learn yet another lesson. I had to develop techniques that used the muscles of my body properly. If my effort was slowed down by sore, aching muscles, my production was limited. The proper use of muscles allowed me to fully make a determined effort. I was a successful cotton picker.

Effort helped me on the football field, too. Although I had a great desire to play the game, I was small and slow. Trying harder and giving more effort seemed to be the way to succeed, just as in the cotton field. I would be the first one in any line and would do whatever football task I was asked to do. I gave full effort from the time the ball snapped until the whistle blew and, most of the time, effort beyond that. Effort, I have found, is a common denominator. If someone has great talent and ability and gives less effort, someone with less talent and ability who gives greater effort can match the one with the greater talent.

Mike Singletary is a great example of this. When he finished his senior year at Baylor University he had been all-American three years in a row and defensive player of the year in the SWC for three straight years, and had won the Davey O'Brien Award for two consecutive years. But even after he had accomplished all this, some of the pro clubs considered him—at just a shade under six feet tall— too short. Some of the professional teams, relying on computerized guidelines for the physical statistics desirable for each position, rejected Mike. But in the second round of the draft, he was taken by the Chicago Bears. He became the linebacker for the all-Rookie team in 1981, and the starting linebacker for the Chicago Bears. But he was not satisfied with this. In fact, he was very disappointed because Buddy Ryan, the defensive coach for the Bears, would not allow him to stay in the game on third down. (In the pro ranks, third down is typically a passing down, and a linebacker must become very involved in the defensive secondary. At Baylor, where Mike had competed against running teams, he had not developed the skill a linebacker needs in performing certain pass drops, nor had he developed the ability to back up into a zone, keep his eyes on the quarterback, and break on the football once it was thrown. All of this added up to his not being allowed stay in the game on the third down.)

The summer after Mike's rookie year in the Pros, he came back to Baylor, and we sat down and talked about his not being able to play on third down. The resolve in his eyes and the determination in his words told me that Mike Singletary was going to do whatever it took to stay on the field on third downs the next year. That summer I witnessed the making of an all-Pro linebacker for the Chicago Bears who went on to become one of the two or three greatest linebackers ever to play in the professional game. Mike Singletary is a shoo-in as a Hall of Famer.

If you've watched Mike play in person or on television, two of his traits have been very evident. One is his intensity—and the television cameras picked up those intense eyes—and the other is his great effort. And that summer of discontent for Mike Singletary was filled with hours of intensity and great effort. At seven o'clock in the morning he would start using our projection room to look for hours at film from the games he had played in college and in his rookie year, evaluating every step and every move. Then he would go out onto the practice field and practice for hours.

Sometimes I would look out and he would be on the field, by himself, lining up against an imaginary offense. On the snap of the imaginary ball, breaking to the proper depth and in the proper position for his break, imagining that the ball was thrown to the right or to the left, and immediately breaking on that ball, Mike worked—hour after hour, day after day throughout the summer. While others enjoyed their summer playing golf or swimming, Mike Singletary gave great effort so that the very next year, Buddy Ryan would leave him in on third downs. The rest is history.

Effort is a personal thing. It embodies commitment and dedication, but above all, a willingness to work above and beyond the call of duty. If we can learn from Mike Singletary the value of effort and apply that to the daily tasks that we're confronted with, we can be successful beyond all of our dreams.

Another of the people who exemplified the value of effort is my father, William (Bill) Garland Teaff. One of the heroes in my life, he graduated from high school just as the Great Depression in America started. Because there was no money to go to school, and because little Grant Garland Teaff was born, Bill Teaff started to work to support his family. My dad worked for the Works Progress Administration—the WPA—a government-sustained program. And when that job ran out, he did something that has been a motivation to me since I first learned of it as a small child. Just off the square in Snyder, Texas, there was a large service station combined with a garage for automobile mechanics. It also served as a bus station and an automobile dealership, and just across the street, the owner of the station had what was known as a tourist court. (We call them motels now.)

One morning, when the day manager of Stinson Motor Company arrived to open the doors, a young man was seated outside the station on a stack of old tires. It was Bill Teaff. When the manager opened the door and started to sweep the driveway, my father picked up a broom and joined in. All morning long, anything that needed to be done my father did without being told. About eleven that morning, Ollie Stinson, the owner of that station, saw my father scurrying around filling up automobiles, washing windshields, fixing truck flats, changing batteries.

Mr. Stinson asked the day manager, "*Who* is that?"

The manager said, "Well, I don't know. I thought you sent him here to work."

Mr. Stinson approached my father, and asked, "Who are you?"

"I'm Bill Teaff."

"What are you doing here?"

"I'm working."

"Who hired you?"

"No one."

With a puzzled look on his face, Mr. Stinson asked, "Well then, why in the world would you be working when no one told you to?"

My father said, "I wanted you to know what a good worker I am. I figured if you discovered that, you would be sure to hire me."

Mr. Stinson did, and my father stayed with that business for more than twenty years, becoming the general manager and part owner. Throughout my life, my father has always worked, and has always given great effort. He taught me at an early age that if something's worth doing, it's worth doing right, and if someone pays you to do a job, it's your responsibility to do it to the best of your ability. My father is now 83 years old and still works full-time. Born in a dugout in Oklahoma Territory in 1910 and brought to Texas in the back of a wagon pulled by four horses, he now runs a computerized register in a White's Auto Store in Snyder, Texas. And he gives the same effort to that computerized register as he did to that broom in Ollie Stinson's service station.

In the classroom environment, a prepared teacher is evidence of effort. And since I believe that effort must be talked about, I think that as a teacher it's up to me to make examples of those who give effort in and out of the classroom. I think it's helpful to point out success stories where effort made the difference, to demonstrate that effort can become a way of life that ensures a measure of success, to tell students to adopt as their motto: *If it's to be, it's up to me!*

Errors

I've made many mistakes, but one that stands out in my mind occurred when I was a small child living on Avenue S, in Snyder, Texas. We had a small house with a small barn and a lot behind it. On that lot, we had some chickens for eggs and a cow for milk. Although I was only six years old, it was my job to gather the eggs and to milk the cow. But doing those jobs subtracted from my time with the guys in the neighborhood, who for several days we had been building a cave on the vacant lot next to our house.

This particular day, after gathering the eggs, I ran to the barn, put the stool down, sat on it, put some feed in the cow's trough so that she would be still, and proceeded to milk her. But time was running out. I was in a hurry to rejoin the group, as we were going to finish the cave that day. And I had only a quarter of a pail of milk. This meant I was about a quarter way through the milking. Nonetheless, I rushed back into the house, placed the pail and the eggs on the cabinet by the sink, and started to run out the door. My mom walked up just about the time I set the pail down, and as I was about to head out the door, called my name, asking, "What happened to the milk?"

I was tempted to say, "I spilled the milk," but thought better of it. Instead, I said, "Well, that's all there was today, Mom."

She said, "No, that's not all there was. You take the pail and go back out and finish the job."

That error in judgment cost me the opportunity to go out and play with my friends. When I returned to the house with the pail almost full, my mother sent me to my room. As I closed the door behind me, her words echoed in my ears, "It's a good thing you didn't compound your mistake by not telling the truth."

As a coach, I know the value of being error-free, and it's something I always stressed with my players. If they could turn in a performance that was error-free, there was a good chance that they'd win the game. In the academic classroom, though, I realize that being able to cope with errors and even failures is a valuable skill, and one that needs to be developed in students so they can learn to rise from failure, as did Jay Jeffrey after he threw that bad pass, or his brother Neal when he threw the ball out of bounds. While we should strive to be error-free, it's true that everyone makes mistakes, and it's important that they get right back up and keep on trying.

"I agree with that," said Cheryl. "I think it's far more important to teach students that they can make mistakes, but that they have to learn to pick themselves up and go on afterward. I think it's important that they see us making mistakes. If they never see us making mistakes, when it happens to them, they're going to say, 'Oh, no, what am I going to do?' Instead of that, I think they need to see us acknowledge our errors and then set about making them right."

"Another thing I think a teacher should do is say, 'I'm sorry,'" said Sharon. "If I find I've messed up, that's the first thing I do. I believe it really helps the kids to realize that I'm just human."

"I do, too," said JoAnn. "And I apologize in front of the whole class. I want them to know I messed up and I'm sorry. Teaching has changed so much in the last twenty years. Students are no longer receiving an education at home, not even in respect and other basics, so we have to be sure to teach them these things."

While students need to learn to continue their efforts after making a mistake, they also need to realize that everyone *will* make mistakes and fail, but that no one should be satisfied with a failure or mistake. Mistakes hurt more than just the individual making the mistake. Errors can be costly to your friends, to your family, to your teammates. Many times, penalties imposed after a mistake are more harmful to others than to the one who made the mistake.

I learned this lesson through participating in football practice. I was an offensive lineman in high school, and one afternoon in practice I had become very intense about trying to defeat someone on the defensive side of the field. (He'd probably gotten the better of me earlier in the scrimmage.) When our offensive team came to the line of scrimmage, just prior to the ball snapping, I moved across the neutral zone and heard the whistle blow. It was Coach Kizer, my high-school line coach. His face was red and I could tell he was very upset. The wind must have been blowing that day because I remember he entwined his hand in my jersey and pulled me up close to his face so I could hear him over the wind.

He asked, "Do you realize what you just did?"

I said, "Yes sir. I jumped offsides."

He asked, "Do you know what that means?"

I said, "Yes sir. That's a 5-yard penalty."

Coach turned me around and pointed five yards behind the line of scrimmage, and asked, "Do you think in your wildest imagination that the official is going to move you five yards behind the team for the penalty?"

I said, "Well, no, sir. He..."

And then it dawned on me that the point being made was that the entire team was being penalized because I had made a mistake. In a ball game, that 5-yard penalty could have cost us the game. A team can be well-prepared, indeed, a team can be better than the other team and still lose because someone makes a mistake. If it's true on the field of athletics, it's true in our homes, in our classrooms, in business, and in everyday life. Striving to become error-free is not only for ourselves but for those around us about whom we care.

Eliminate mistakes.

III.
The Principles of Success

Doing the right thing isn't always the easiest thing to do. And it does not ensure immediate success. But the overall concept ultimately leads to success in all you do.

—Grant Teaff

I always tell my students, "Ask yourself before you do something if your parents would be proud of what you're about to do. If you can answer 'Yes,' go ahead and do it."

—Don Bridgeman, high-school teacher,
Flossmoor, Illinois

INTRODUCTION
Principle Defined

The dictionary's definition of a principle is "an accepted or professed rule of action or conduct; a fundamental, a primary law of truth, or a basis of conduct or management." My own personal definition is that a principle is a basic, consistent truth that will apply in every instance. I have used what I call the principles of success in every area of my own personal life: as a player and student, as a coach, as a husband and father, as a person involved in business, and as a person managing others.

There are certain basics in anything we do. In athletics, if you find yourself unable to achieve the success you had hoped for, you need to review the basic techniques of the sport you are playing. These techniques form a foundation on which you can feel comfortable and which allows you to concentrate on building other skills. The basic techniques are things you do naturally, things you've worked on and repeated so many times they have become second nature. But if you stray from them, you may find your efforts are in vain. So it is with these basic principles of success. I use them in my own life, talk about them daily, enhance my understanding of them, apply them all the time, and then recognize and applaud them when I see them in action.

10.
Do the Right Thing

Recently a young man by the name of Spike Lee made a movie called, "Do the Right Thing." Long before that movie title was used, it was a principle of success. This principle was hammered into me as a child by my parents' repeated response to my questions about how I should handle certain things. Their response was always, "Grant, do the right thing." When I would ask a question about how to handle a situation that had come up on the playground or in the classroom, the answer would normally be, "Well, just do the right thing." Sometimes I found this frustrating, but I soon realized that my parents were giving me a chance to make a decision on my own. And the ownership of what I was about to do was always prefaced by the words, "Do the right thing."

With that thought in the back of my mind each time I answered someone, responded to them in some way, or actually did something as a reaction, I continually felt a burden to try to do the right thing. To help me decide what the right thing was, I developed a mental checklist. That checklist has stood me in good stead in my relationships with others, in my role as a husband and father, and certainly as a leader. It included the following questions:

Is it fair? Is it honest? Is it loyal? Is it kind? Is it considerate?

In other situations, the questions would become: Am I being helpful? Am I being unselfish? Am I being respectful? After I began to teach and coach, I realized my role was also to serve others with my talents and abilities, and I summed up all the questions in that mental checklist by simply asking myself if I was approaching each situation and reacting to it with a servant's heart.

Doing the right thing isn't always the easiest thing to do. Sometimes it involves making a hard judgment call. And sometimes trying to do the right thing doesn't turn out the way we want it to. Just doing the right thing does not ensure immediate success. But the overall concept ultimately leads to success in everything you do. The thing I like about using this concept in my life is that when I put my head on the pillow at night, I can close my eyes and go to sleep knowing that during that day I have consciously and subconsciously tried to do the right thing in every circumstance.

Since this principle has worked well in my life, I've always tried to teach it to my student/athletes. To do this, I've used the technique of emphasis—one of the great tools of teaching—throughout my years of coaching. When you place emphasis on something, your audience may alter their perception: The point of emphasis can become important to them because you're stressing it. Similarly, if you repeat something enough, it has a tendency to become ingrained in the individuals being taught. I decided that I could use the techniques of emphasis and repetition to teach the concept of doing the right thing.

One of the ways I stressed this concept—and this can be done to teach many concepts, values, and mental approaches—was to build on a particular value each day. First, I would put the message, "Do the right thing," in a conspicuous place, so that the players would see it many times a day. The message was on the daily handouts, and on a placard above the door. Later in my career I even secured an electronic, lighted machine that rotated the message. That way, when my players walked into the area to begin to dress for the afternoon's workouts and meetings, the thought would be repeated over and over again on the electric signboard, "Do the right thing. Do the right thing. Do the right thing."

To build on this, at the beginning of the meeting time before practice, I would simply explain what "doing the right thing" actually meant. I would try to keep it brief, but I'd make two or three points about *doing the right thing* as a way to achieve success, perhaps by citing an example or two to which the players could relate. Next, the position coaches would emphasize *doing the right thing* in their meetings with the players by giving their own viewpoints on what *doing the right thing* meant.

Then the phrase would be mentioned throughout the practice, and at the end of the practice I would talk with the team for about five minutes, reviewing what we'd done and reiterating the point of the day. I might well use something that had happened in the practice to illustrate what *doing the right thing* on the practice field meant.

Finally, I would ask each of the players to consciously think about *doing the right thing* and to come up with his definition of what that actually meant before the next day, when I might call on him to explain it to the squad.

When they came in the next day, the players would see the same signs, but now every time they saw a coach, trainer, or manager, that individual would say in greeting, "Hi. Do the right thing." In the team meeting I would call on two or three guys to give their definition of what it meant to *do the right thing* in all circumstances. And I'd call on someone else to explain how always consciously *doing the right thing* can help you be successful.

In position meetings, the coaches would relate an incident in their own lives where they had done the right thing at the right time and it had helped them to reach a certain level of success. I would conclude the practice with further emphasis on the point, and ask each one of the players in his greetings to other students on campus, with his girlfriend on the telephone, and with his teammates, to close each conversation with the words, "Do the right thing."

We were beginning to build momentum in our emphasis. Underneath the sign that said, "Do the right thing," we now would attach the words, "Be fair." Now the whole day's procedure would be repeated, using fairness as the point of emphasis. By repeating this procedure day after day over a period of time, the points emphasized became second nature to the players and coaches alike.

The next point of emphasis we would make might be "Look before you leap," or better still, "Think before you act," and we would use similar techniques to emphasize this point. The concept of thinking before you act is something that should be ingrained in everyone, no matter what their field of endeavor. When you plan a major purchase, it's advisable to wait twenty-four hours after you've decided what you want before actually making the purchase. This is really to give you a cooling-off period to make sure that you are doing the right thing in expending your money.

When I read about that 24-hour waiting period recently, it reminded me of something I first heard at a Rotary Club, where I was asked to give a speech early in my career. The luncheon began with a prayer, the Pledge of Allegiance, and the singing of the national anthem. Then those present repeated something else that impressed me greatly. It's called *The Four-Way Test of Things We Think, Say, and Do,* and consists of four questions.

The Principles of Success: Do the Right Thing

1. Is it the truth?
2. Is it fair to all concerned?
3. Will it build goodwill and better friendships?
4. Will it be beneficial to all concerned?

Rotary International has been asking its members to live by the Four-Way Test since 1946, and I think it would be great if we would all do the same. It may seem hokey, but if everybody did the right thing, there would be no wars, no crime, and we would have a much better world in which to live.

> *Wade, who teaches Applied Math and Geometry to ninth through twelfth graders, said, "I'm a former salesman, and subscribe to the technique of building on a theme one hundred percent. I think it's something that I really need to do in my classroom, that I'm not really successful at—yet. My big job is not teaching. It's motivating the students. I know the material, but if the students are not motivated, they're not going to accept the material."*
>
> *Don said, "I've been teaching and coaching for the last twenty-four years, so I found this really interesting. I don't know that I necessarily build on a theme in the same way, but I do make a big deal about doing the right thing. In the classroom situation, I teach Industrial Education, where the kids have more freedom to move around and there's the possibility of getting hurt, so I always tell them, 'Ask yourself before you do something if your parents would be proud of what you're about to do. If you can answer 'Yes,' go ahead and do it. But if you have to answer, 'No,' then you know*

you're not doing the right thing. I teach in a large open room where we have a welding section, machine tools, and a computer-operated manufacturing lab. Not everyone is visible, so I have to be able to trust the kids to do the right thing."

11.
Find a Purpose

As a child, I found it very hard to do the chores that I was asked to do because I saw no purpose in doing many of them. But the tasks I wanted to do and had a good reason for doing, I found easier to do. I'm not alone in this situation. We need to find a purpose in all things if we are to do them well. History shows that when armies fight for a cause and clearly know their purpose, they fight with more resolve and, in most cases, greater success.

The need for an answer to the question, "Why?" has shaped the future of many an individual. As a parent, I learned that asking my children to do something simply because I said so was not the best way to get it done. Human nature is to want to know why, and I certainly was asked that question many times by my three daughters. Pretty soon I got smarter than the equipment, so to speak, and began to realize that if I could place a reason, a purpose, or a cause with the project that I was asking them to do, there was certainly a better chance of its getting done.

We've all heard of the explorer going to the top of Mt. Everest and saying that the reason he climbed the mountain was simply because it was there. We know that voyagers have crossed the oceans on large sailing ships and in one-man crafts simply because the oceans were there. And certainly the exploration of space has been spurred on by the simple fact that it is there. But not everyone is motivated by this. Most people need a cause or purpose.

The Biblical story of David and Goliath is a prime example of someone seeing a purpose in doing something that no one else at the time could see. No member of the army of the king of Israel would fight single-handedly a giant of a person by the name of Goliath. This giant was a trained warrior, and nobody wanted to take him on. But a young guy who worked with sheep heard about the situation and wanted to try. His name was David, and he saw a purpose in defeating Goliath. The purpose he saw was two-fold: He would have the opportunity to become influential and successful, and to save his nation, two great motivating factors to do a job. Because this young man saw a purpose in fighting someone he really had no business fighting, he was so motivated that he ultimately won, and gave us a great lesson about the importance of having a purpose.

"Since my students often have an 'it doesn't matter to me' attitude, I have to try and tie whatever concept I'm teaching them to their own lives somehow," said Cindy. "I'm a science teacher, so it's easy enough to do. For example, I might try to explain what would happen later in their lives if they didn't know this concept. And I'll tell them stories of what happened when someone else didn't know the concept. Also, I'll tell them that what I'm teaching is something they may need to know if their mother or father is hospitalized, to understand

what the medical staff is telling them. This makes them understand that there is a purpose in learning certain things, and they can relate it to their lives."

"A lot of our migrant students come to school only because it's the law," said Joyce Pinkard, a bilingual teacher in Madera, California. "Many of our students' families believe that the students should be out there in the fields, helping them earn a living. So we not only have to show them the relationship of everything we're teaching to the real world, but also we have to give them a reason to come to school other than because it's the law. I think it's critical to let the kids know how the lesson you're teaching is going to be applied in their lives. I don't think it helps to tell students, 'Well, you'll find out later how you'll use that.'"

Through the years, the teams I've coached that have been very successful were all driven by a purpose or a cause. I'm not talking about the personal goals and motivation that drive an individual, but rather the cause that pulls a team together and allows it to be successful. The cause has to be overriding, and it has to be one that constantly motivates and drives the team unit. I could name hundreds of examples, but I keep remembering two, one of which occurred at the beginning of my career at Baylor University, and then one that happened in the very last game I coached.

In the summer of 1974, our football team was coming off a 2 and 9 season in the fall of 1973. We were picked dead last in the Southwest Conference, and many did not think we would win a game because our first three opponents in 1974—Oklahoma, Missouri, and Oklahoma State—were all listed in the top ten teams in the country.

Then, coming from a position of not having won a conference game the year before, we had to play the outstanding teams in the state of Texas. Just as the season started in 1974, *Texas Monthly*, a magazine widely read across the state, had on its cover a staged picture showing cheerleaders from the University of Texas and yell leaders from Texas A&M University standing over a casket, looking down with sorrow at what was supposed to be the remains of the private schools in Texas. The associated article proclaimed that private schools in Texas were dead and should be buried. And, it said, the one that was the "deadest" was Baylor University. That article flew in the face of our individual pride and pride in our university. It was an insult, and one that our football team took to heart. It gave us a cause.

Of course, many ingredients go into making a successful season. I'm not saying that every day our team talked about winning a conference championship because a magazine had said that Baylor should give up football. But I do say an overriding motivation was consistently present after the article was published. That motivation led to our first conference championship in fifty years, and the defeat of our arch-rivals and the perennial SWC winner, the University of Texas, whom we beat in a come-from-behind effort.

But the crowning irony of the season occurred at the Cotton Bowl, at a team dinner with the media. By chance, I presume, the individual who had written the article for *Texas Monthly* was sitting at my table. What satisfaction I felt when I leaned over and whispered a few words to him! The puzzled look on his face reflected the fact that he couldn't understand what I had meant when I said: "Thanks for the great article last September."

The second example occurred when Baylor University was playing the University of Arizona in the John Hancock Bowl. Arizona had one of the outstanding teams in the nation, and we had made it to the Bowl by defeating the University of Texas in the last regular game of the season. Unfortunately, circumstances were not the most ideal under which to coach a game, since Baylor had hired a new football coach on the Monday after our final game with Texas. A week later, when Texas A&M defeated Texas, we were extended an invitation to play Arizona in the John Hancock Bowl. Most of the members of my staff had not been retained by the new coach. So they had to deal with knowing they would not be part of the future of a program they had worked so hard to build. And now they were being asked to come back and help prepare a team to play one of the better teams in the nation! The professional job they did was outstanding, but we needed something to help us overcome the Arizona team, whose players were bigger and probably stronger. Overall they were faster, had a much better record, and were supposed to win by a couple of touchdowns. We needed something. But what?

When we arrived at the Bowl site in El Paso, the Arizona team began to talk about the weakness of the Southwest Conference. Then, at a team party later in the week, their feelings came out in a skit, and it was the best thing that could have happened to our football team. Trying to be funny, the participants in the Arizona skit belittled our team primarily because we were a member of the SWC, a struggling conference not viewed by members of the Pacific Athletic Conference as a power conference.

Now, any team worth its salt has a desire to win every game it plays, but on certain occasions, more is needed than a desire to win. This was one of those occasions, and in the lack of respect shown for our team and for the SWC, we found the purpose we needed to spur us on. The players talked about it every day. Their resolve to work hard and their desire to win had been magnified.

When the game was over and our team rushed to the middle of the field to receive the trophy as champions

111

of the John Hancock Bowl, they spontaneously began to chant, "SWC! SWC!" Southwest Conference. There were smiles on every face, and the comments of our players after the game reinforced the fact that Arizona had made a bad mistake by giving this Baylor team a cause: the cause of a maligned Southwest Conference.

> Don said, "I worked in industry for ten years before becoming a teacher, so it's been easy for me to explain to kids why we're doing a certain thing. I deal with certain behaviors by telling students, 'Your actions just now would have caused you to be fired from a job.' We talk about punctuality and attendance, respect for the teacher being parallel to respect for a boss, and it's easy for me to relate whatever scenario we're involved in to real life. The kids respond very well to this, because at the end of their time with me, I get them jobs. If they're not punctual, or are disrespectful, they know I won't put my name alongside theirs on a recommendation form. They have a clear idea of what my expectations are."
>
> "This year," said Wade, "since we started teaching Applied Math rather than general math, I've seen a big change. At age 52, I'm retraining myself to teach in a hands-on manner. Today we were in a geometry section of the Applied Math book, and the students had to build different triangles using straws. Tomorrow, we're going to be laying out the foundation for a home, and they're going to have to apply the principles they used in making the triangles. So math is becoming more relevant to them. They're finding it really has a purpose."

Bob Roth, a math teacher in Dexter, Michigan, said, "In graphing, I make the point that when you're learning about how two numbers can put a point on a graph, you're also learning how two numbers can help put a rocket ship on the moon. In explaining algebra, instead of talking about plus and minus numbers, I've had really good success with telling my students that minus is money they owe, and plus is money they have. When the kids have to deal with the concept of minus five, plus three, for example, I'll tell them, 'Now think about it. You owe somebody five dollars, and you only have three. What will the situation be when you pay them all you can? You'll either have money left or you'll still owe some.' Almost to a student, they can figure it out."

Individuals are just as driven by a purpose and cause as is a team. There are hundreds of examples of people who have made millions of dollars or accomplished athletic feats beyond imagination. But one individual who did neither has always stood out for me, and that is Dr. Albert Schweitzer, a doctor who could have achieved professional and financial success beyond most people's imaginations, but chose instead to follow a simple cause: to serve. Dr. Schweitzer touched and changed lives while giving his own to a cause.

Purposes and causes fuel the engines that drive us. Self-fulfillment and satisfaction from serving a purpose or a cause greater than we are is one of the greatest motivating factors known to man. It certainly has been a factor in my life. My longevity at Baylor, a small private school, impressed some and amazed others. The media particularly could not understand why I would stay at Baylor when I had the opportunity to coach in large major universities across the nation. The point they never understood was that I believed in what I was doing at Baylor, and I served a broader cause than that of just coaching football. I believe in the type of education that Baylor gives, and I was driven by the fact that Baylor was considered by many to be a "have not." I wanted to prove that more could be done with less, and in the right way. My desire was that people across this nation would look to Baylor University with respect because it was graduating the student athletes who formed a successful football program, a program that had been built with integrity.

12.
Develop Successful Habits

Aristotle wrote, "We are what we repeatedly do." Excellence, then, is not an act, but a habit. Over the years, I've found that habits can be developed, but they also can be lost over time if not practiced. In his best-selling book, *The Seven Habits of Highly Effective People*, Stephen R. Covey defined habits as "the intersection of knowledge, skill, and desire." Creating a habit requires work in all three dimensions. Think of a golf swing. Before you develop a golf swing, you need to find out what constitutes a correct swing. To find that out you look at the success of others, at physiological research, at timing and speed, and at the effect of matter on matter. Then you have to build on that knowledge by using your physical capabilities to achieve the swing you want. You also need a strong motivation and the desire to practice your swing over and over again so that it will become a habit.

The habits we develop determine our behavior and our style, which ultimately affect the success of our chosen career. I've found that successful individuals have formed the habit of doing the things that those who fail just don't like to do. The successful coaches I've observed over the years were successful more because of their philosophies, attitudes, and habits than because of any particular offense, defense, or technique that they used.

As Samuel Johnson said, "The chains of habit are generally too small to be felt until they are too strong to be broken." So it could be said that we first of all make our habits, and then our habits make us. I very much like this suggestion by Grenville Kleiser: "You set your destiny by what you make of yourself. Be an early student of yourself. Learn by frequent self-examination to appraise and improve your attitudes, aspirations, and habits."

As teachers, we can influence our students for the better if we are first students of ourselves.

The Habit of Simplicity

The habit of simplicity is the first of four habits that must be developed to achieve success. The acronym KISS, or "Keep it simple, sir," sums this up. (KISS originally stood for "Keep it simple, stupid." I consider the word "stupid" to be demeaning and usually irrelevant, so I have developed a habit of not using it.) The philosophy of KISS was reinforced for me several years ago when I was fortunate enough to be a speaker at a large salesmanship convention in Dallas. The speaker who preceded me was one of the most outstanding in the profession, and made many good points. One of them stood out enough for me to write down. I believe it is applicable not only in sales but in everything we do. I certainly know it is applicable in the game of football. What I wrote down was, "The power of your sales presentation will always lie in its simplicity."

Believing something and then hearing someone as renowned as Dr. Kenneth McFarland verify what you believe is truly exciting. I strive for simplicity in my life. When I speak, I try to make simple points that are easily understood. I try not to elaborate too much. Even the philosophies of offense and defense that I used through my years of coaching were predicated on simplicity. I always believed that the simpler the game plan, the more easily it could be executed by the team. The simpler an explanation or demonstration, the easier it is to understand. Simplifying eliminates a lot of opportunities for misunderstanding.

"I think simplicity is essential," said Bob. "If my lesson goes really well, and I say everything the way I want to say it, nobody interrupts me and everybody seems to get it, I feel really good. And that usually happens when I've broken down a concept into three simple points. If I do it simply, the students can remember it."

"In teaching bilingual students, we have to teach simply," said Joyce. "While our students are learning to speak English, they also need to stay at grade level in their other studies. So we teach them in their native language until they're ready to transfer to a regular classroom. Simplicity is essential."

The Habit of Planning

Experts claim that you can increase your efficiency by at least 25 percent if you plan, and I believe it. You simply cannot be organized unless you plan to be organized. You cannot accomplish all the things that have to be done within the day unless you plan. Then, at the end of the day, you can go back and evaluate how effective your plan was. Planning, though, is not enough. You also have to prioritize the things that are important. If you don't, you may spend too much time on the least important item that you planned to accomplish. One of the most satisfying experiences is to make a plan and to execute the plan successfully. The other is to pass on your beliefs to those you love and see them at work in their lives. I remember walking out to get in my car to go to work one morning and noticing my youngest daughter, Layne, still sitting in her car. I walked to her car, tapped on the window, and asked her, "Are you having car trouble?" She rolled down the window, looked at me with her beautiful smile, and said, "Oh, no. I'm planning my day. I'm making my 'do' list."

I felt a warm sense of gratification when she said this, because I realized that something I believed in had rubbed off on one of the most important people in my life.

In 1992, our football team was playing Georgia Tech at homecoming. During the week, our coaches observed that the Georgia Tech defense was very fast in its pursuit of the football. In other words, the defensive team keyed on the football itself, and had a tendency to quickly leave their areas of responsibility, particularly in the secondary. That made them very vulnerable to a misdirection type of pass. The staff agreed to put in an old play that we had used in previous years. We called it the Texas Special because we had first used it against the University of Texas. The players became familiar with it during the week, and we executed it many times during practice.

On the Friday night prior to the ball game, my three daughters arrived from out of town for homecoming. My middle daughter, Tracy, is always interested in the game plan for the next day, and never fails to ask me about it. She'll particularly ask me if there are any trick plays in the plan. On this particular Friday night, I said, "Yes. You remember the old Texas Special?" And of course, she did. She proceeded to explain it to Tammy's two children, Josh and Jessy, aged 6 and 3 respectively, and to Layne and Donell. Upon hearing the explanation, Donell said politely, "That play won't work."

(Now, if some football fan had been eavesdropping on this conversation, I'm sure they would've been in shock. Two children, four adult females, and a coach were discussing the game plan and a specific play, and one of the females was proclaiming that the play wouldn't work!)

Tracy believed in the play, and she set out to demonstrate to Donell just how it *would* work. Tracy lined Jessy up as the center, took her position as the quarterback, appointed Layne the wide receiver on one side, Tammy the wide receiver on the opposite side, and Josh the tailback. With everyone in place, Tracy turned and pitched the ball to Josh, who ran to his right, handed it off to his mother coming back to her left, who then pitched the ball to Tracy the quarterback. In the meantime, Layne, the wide receiver, had gone deep through the den and into a small dining area waiting for the long pass. She reached and grabbed the ball just before it hit the china cabinet, and all the girls, Josh and Jessy, started jumping up and down. The play was successful.

The next day we were behind in the fourth quarter. Georgia Tech had been gaining momentum in this quarter, had mounted a comeback, and was now leading. We started a drive, and about mid-field, the Texas Special was called. As the wide receiver went into the end zone with the ball for the touchdown that won the game, jubilation broke out on the fields and in the stands. When the game was over and I walked off the field, I saw all my daughters, as well as Josh, Jessy, and Donell, jumping up and down. Tracy was yelling, "Our play worked! We won! Our play worked! We won!"

"Before this year," said Wade, "I used to rely on a body of teaching experience I had acquired over the years, but this year, I've been planning my lessons pretty carefully. I've had

*to work hard to teach myself and my students
to get involved in this new type of hands-on
learning, but it's working well. I have two
ninth-grade classes who are not in the top
section academically, yet in those classes I have
forty kids who are excited about math!*

*"I go over and over the things I teach in
my mind before I teach, and the more I do that,
the better the class goes."*

*"I plan my lessons in my head," said
Bob. "I also find I have to change my plans if
the students are not responding to the lesson
I'm teaching. For example, this week, the
students had gotten to a point where they
didn't want to do any of the lessons in the book,
so I went down to a room where there were
some unused computers—unused only because
they are so old and user-unfriendly—and in
one day I had my classroom set up with six
computers and was running them off individual disks. On the first day I wasn't really
sure where I was going with it, but two days
after I set up the computers, I had everybody
working again. Now I'm planning like crazy
trying to keep ahead of where the kids are
going. It's great."*

The Habit of Practice

Frank Leahy was one of the great coaches of all
time. A consummate winner, he coached for the University
of Notre Dame. Frank Leahy's plan for success was all-
encompassing, but he stressed the importance of practice.
His philosophy was, "Learn from others, strive to be a

perfectionist. Believe in overcompensation. Never follow the line of least resistance. Practice the correct way, not the easy way. These attitudes overcome the opposition and bring victory."

Practice goes with planning like jam goes with bread. They work so well together. "Plan your practice and practice your plan" is an adage directly from coaching, and is applicable to almost anything we do, particularly in teaching. The reason a good golfer doesn't have to think about a correct backswing or the speed of the head of the driver coming through the ball is that he has practiced it so many times that it has become second nature.

A willingness to put in seventeen hours a day of practice for many years allows some people to be called "genius". Michelangelo put it a different way. He said, "If people only knew how hard I worked to gain mastery, the performance wouldn't seem wonderful at all."

In *Positive Power for Successful Salesmen*, the story is told of Fritz Kreisler, a world-renowned violinist, who had a similar outlook. One evening after he had finished a concert, he was approached by an elderly lady who said, "Mr. Kreisler, I would give my life to be able to play a violin like that."

"Madam," said Kreisler, "I did."

"We practice all the time," Joyce said. "We have to. Life is so much more simple in Mexico—for example, some of our children have never even had access to a newspaper—that we find we have to teach even the most basic concepts, like adding sales tax to a purchase. Our area is largely rural, and the main industry is agriculture. Many of the students' families are field workers. We have to plan carefully, because

*our kids start in our program all through the
year, not just in September. So we practice the
same things over and over, all year round."*

*"When students bring in their home-
work," said Wade, "I don't look at how many
they got right and how many they got wrong.
Rather, I ask them, 'Did you try all the problems?' If they say yes, then I verify it, and give
them one hundred percent for the homework.
Then I tell the kids, 'Okay, let's look at the ones
you got wrong and find out about the mistakes.
If you don't take time to correct them, you're
practicing wrong. It'd be like a basketball
player playing with a football all day, and then
playing a basketball game that night. You're
not going to be successful if you practice doing
the wrong thing.'"*

I don't believe that success is a matter of luck. I
think it's a matter of work, work, and work. I've always
said to my coaching staff and our team, "Our opponents
may be bigger, stronger, faster, or even more intelligent,
but they will not outwork us." All the principles and
characteristics and habits we've talked about have their
place, but none can bear fruit until hard work—work that
is properly directed, with a proper goal—occurs.

Work has always been important to me. My father
gave me a work ethic that is unstoppable. Of all the gifts
we receive from our parents—from genes and philosophy
to observation—there are two for which I am immensely
grateful. My mom was always the positive one, the one who
helped me really believe in myself. But my dad inspires me
with his work ethic, and always has. I take great pride in
the fact that Dad is 83 years old this year (1994) and
continues to work full time.

Dad is also a stickler for doing things right. He used to tell me, "If it's worth doing, it's worth doing right." In his opinion, you can't work too hard. So I started pretty young, holding my first full-time job in the summer when I was ten years old, working for a truck-tire company. Since that time I've always had a job, whether I was in school or out of school. While I was in college, I taught swimming lessons and ran a swimming pool in the summers, and during the year, besides playing football and getting my degrees, I worked in radio and television stations.

I remember when I was going into my sophomore year in high school and Coaches Speedy Moffat and Mule Kizer really were working us hard to get us in shape for the season. One day, we evidently didn't give the kind of effort we should have. So, after we ran our regular amount of conditioning following practice, Coach Moffat lined us up and started running us again. We ran for quite a long time. When we finished we were all exhausted. One of my teammates informed his father about the very hard work that day, and the young man's father called Coach Moffat at home and threatened to physically fight him over the matter. A few years later, Coach Moffat told me that the very next day he'd gone down to the bank, where he'd run into my dad. Coach Moffat said to my father, "I guess you're upset about the hard work Grant did yesterday after practice."

My dad looked at him squarely in the eyes and said, "Why, of course not. There's just not any way you can work him too hard. Pour it on him."

Coach Moffat was impressed with the mentality in our home, and I can only say to my father, "Thank you. Thank you for that work ethic you gave me."

The Habit of Enthusiasm

Samuel Goldwyn, the movie producer and head of the studio that still bears his name, once said, "I have found enthusiasm for work and life to be the most precious ingredient in any recipe for successful living. And the greatest feature of this ingredient is that it is available to everyone within him[her]self." Enthusiasm is contagious. It is a mind-set, an approach to life that differs from most. It's developed by a positive outlook on the future, believing that good things are going to happen, and then excitedly pursuing your goals.

If you are excited about something, you want to get right to it. Procrastination occurs because of a lack of enthusiasm. You put off projects you're not enthusiastic about. Enthusiasm for projects begins with an enthusiasm for life, an excitement about the wonder of life itself and the joy of living.

Do you ever wonder what happens when enthusiasm meets enthusiasm? Well, let me tell you.

Bill Lane and I played junior college ball together and became fast friends. He went on to have a very successful career as a Texas high-school coach, winning something like thirty-three games in a row and a couple of state championships. In 1969, when I accepted the challenge to try to bring a winning season to Angelo State University, I called Bill Lane to see if he would be willing to join my coaching staff. He came with a tremendous amount of confidence and enthusiasm, and it was contagious. Bill coached with me for three years at Angelo State, then joined me at Baylor for twenty-two years, so we were together for a total of twenty-five years. Throughout that entire time, no coach I had was more enthusiastic than Bill Lane. He loved the game of football, and was excited about coaching and about life. He was one of the few coaches who really got excited about recruiting. This paid off handsomely for Baylor.

In January of 1977, Bill kept talking to me about a quarterback, Scott Smith, at Highland Park High School in Dallas. Bill was so excited about him. He had watched him work out and had talked to the head coach at Highland Park High, Frank Beaver, who had said all sorts of positive things about Scott. Scott was an outstanding high-school quarterback, but in my opinion didn't have the characteristics of speed or size or strength of arm to be a SWC quarterback. I remember Bill enthusiastically telling me about how Scott would go down to school at 6 a.m. in the summer, crawl through a window of the weight room at Highland Park High, and work out for two hours on weights. Then he would spend eight hours on the field working with various techniques of throwing the ball or executing the option. Finally, at 6 p.m., Scott would go back to the weight room for two more hours of work. Bill Lane knows me pretty well, and he kept saying to me, "If you'll just go meet Scott, you'll give him a scholarship."

Finally, almost reluctantly, I went to Dallas with Bill to meet Scott Smith and his family. Once I got there, I was impressed. Scott sat on the edge of his seat and looked me right in the eye. He answered every question with confidence, and when I said, "I'm going to give you a scholarship," he replied, "You won't be sorry."

I never have been.

Scott brought to Baylor University the same commitment and enthusiasm for life and the game of football that had distinguished him in high school. When he got enthusiastic about something, it was believable because of his values and his work ethic. In August of 1977, for example, Scott had prepared himself to be the starting quarterback at Baylor, although there were three or four guys well ahead of him, guys with a lot more talent and ability to throw the ball. But Scott was the first one on the practice field and the last one to leave. What he lacked in skill, he made up for in technique. I've never seen anybody practice any longer, work any harder, or be more enthusiastic about playing the game than Scott Smith. The second game of the 1977 season, we were to play an undefeated

University of Kentucky team. They were quite good. As a matter of fact, the only game they lost in the season was to the Baylor Bears.

In the two weeks prior to the Kentucky game, our quarterbacks began to fall like flies. One was hurt in practice, a couple in games, and, as we began to prepare for the game against the University of Kentucky, it became obvious to the coaching staff that the only quarterback we were going to have available was little Scott Smith. I remember asking him to stop by my office prior to workout on Monday, at which time I informed him that it looked as if he would be the starting quarterback for the Kentucky game. He looked at me, smiled, and said, "I'll be ready."

Scott's enthusiasm added to our workouts something that had been missing, and then he led us to victory against the University of Kentucky. The same enthusiasm that Scott brought to the preparation and victory, he carried to his next assignment, which was to play defensive back for the Baylor Bears. Scott became the starting strong safety, and was a constant leader on one of the most outstanding defenses that's ever played in the SWC. The defense included such people as Mike Singletary and Van McIlroy, first team all-Americans; Charles Benson and Doak Fields, first-team all-Conference; and Joe Johnson, another Baylor all-Conference performer. But nobody on that team made a greater contribution than Scott Smith. His knowledge of the game, his preparation, and his enthusiasm for practice and the game helped set the 1980 championship team apart.

After Scott graduated, he went into coaching, and was successful as an assistant on the college level and as a high-school head coach. One of my proudest days was the day I hired him to become the secondary coach at Baylor University. He brought the same enthusiasm that had distinguished him earlier to his coaching and his recruiting. If I could bottle and sell Scott Smith's and Bill Lane's enthusiasm for life and the game, I would be a very rich man.

"The very good teachers I know use all four of these habits almost subconsciously," said Don. *"You've got to be enthusiastic. I'm always enthusiastic, and I find that it rubs off on the students. Kids know when you're down. They'll say, 'What's the matter, Mr. Bridgeman?' They're pretty bright and they tune into your moods. As to the practice part, I used to tell the kids, 'Practice makes perfect.' Now I tell them, 'Perfect practice makes perfect.' You've got to practice well.*

"In my lab we have to go over safety, and I encourage the students to develop safety habits such as always putting their safety glasses on, always doing the right thing around a piece of equipment, and so on. And all of that takes practice. We also use the KISS principle. Simplicity is really important."

"I teach in an inner-city area," said Bob, *"where we have young parents, and busy parents, and parents who don't have a lot of education. The key factor is that these people chose to live in an area with the lowest housing costs, and, generally speaking, if they can figure out a way to bring together enough money to buy a more expensive property, they move away. Of course a lot of families have been there forever, and never figured out how to move out. I see young bright kids filled with dreams...who never actually practice or plan or get enthusiastic."*

13.
Take Care of the Little Things

Little things mean a lot. Long before Alexander Graham Bell invented the telephone, a German school teacher called Wilhelm Reiss constructed a telephone. He could use it to send a whistle or hum, but it would not transmit speech. Something was lacking. In his version of the telephone, Reiss did not allow the electrodes to touch. Accidentally, in his quest to make a telephone that would transmit speech, Alexander Graham Bell moved one of the screws 1/1000 of an inch, and speech, articulate and clear, came through. A fraction of an inch made the difference.

I've always contended that little successes lead to big successes. Whenever I had a player who was not progressing and was continually in a failure situation, I would personally find a way for him to experience success. After a couple of days of watching drills, if I'd observed one player being unsuccessful in every drill, I would intentionally change the drill the very next day so that young man could taste success. Many times I've seen that small success in a drill change the confidence and the outlook of an individual so dramatically that he went on to become all-Conference or all-American. Little things mean a lot.

"In the lab, my students have to have some small successes, because they have to make something work and then turn it in as a project," said Don. "At the beginning, I help them a little, show them the right way to do something. Then, when they've had a little success, I'll encourage them to think it through. Then they'll make a mistake, and say, 'Oh, Mr. Bridgeman, I've made a mistake!' They expect me to be upset, but I tell them, 'That's great! Mistakes are great, because now you're learned what not to do. The next time I give you this piece of stock, you're going to do the right thing, or at least you won't make the same mistake. I'm only going to get upset if you don't learn from your mistakes.'

"Then I'll give them another piece of material, and they usually won't make the same mistake again. They'll make other mistakes, but by then they've become successful at doing one particular thing, so they're having small successes all the time."

"I also tell my students that the only people who don't make mistakes are those who are not trying," said Wade. "So I encourage them to realize that by trying, they are achieving something."

"I agree that the students have to experience some small successes," said Joyce. "We give weekly awards to students who have done well. A program we use called AVID [see Appendix]—Advancement Via Individual Determination—targets the middle-achievers. Its aim is to place those kids in college prep classes, and provide a tutoring session for them during the day. Students have to manage their

own time and set their own goals, and it really works. Their successes in AVID prepare them for other successes."

One degree of temperature can make a great difference. For instance, at 211 degrees, water is hot but it does not possess power. In the boiler of a locomotive, it exerts not one ounce of pressure. But at 212 degrees, water becomes live steam, and gives off enough power to haul a mile-long train across a mountain pass. At 211 degrees, the water in that same locomotive is powerless: The fire box may as well be empty and cold. Add one more degree of heat, and it has the power to pull a mile-long train at seventy miles per hour. Little things mean a lot.

Some seemingly little things are really quite big. Take for instance the "three Cs": communication, commitment, and competition. To lead or to be successful, you have to communicate your ideas. When nations communicate, there's less likelihood of war. When companies communicate, they can grow strong together. And when individuals communicate, prejudice, hatred, and differences have a tendency to disappear. Communication can be simple, and does not have to be wordy or long. Three of the greatest examples of communication in recorded history are the Ten Commandments, which contain three hundred words; the Declaration of Independence, which contains two hundred ninety-seven words; and the Gettysburg Address, which contains only two hundred sixty-six words.

Two little things that make the difference in communication are listening and learning. When you meet someone, concentrate on what they're saying. Use word association to remember what they tell you. One of the greatest gifts you can give someone is to *listen* to them. This makes them feel good, since they believe that you think what they're saying is worthwhile. Be sure to *learn* the names of the people you meet. You can do this by concentrating when they tell you who they are and then very quickly repeating their name so it will be ingrained in your mind. Learn about people. The more you learn about someone, the better you know them. The better you know them, the better you understand them and like them. Recognize that there is a lot out there you don't know, and by learning you can improve yourself and your opportunities for success.

Commitment seems small to some people, but it's really large. A revealing question to ask yourself is, "What *are* my commitments?" An honest self-evaluation too often will reveal that we are not committed to very much. The great Green Bay Packer coach, Vince Lombardi, put it in very understandable terms. He said, "Unless a man believes in himself, makes a total commitment to his career, and puts everything he has into it, he will never be successful at anything he undertakes." Coach Lombardi did not simply say, "Make a commitment." His words were, "Make a *total* commitment."

In 1991, I wanted to teach my players how important it was to have a team that was really united and totally committed. It took a little effort, but I came up with an idea that would show them what I meant. At the beginning of the season, at our very first team meeting, I prepared a demonstration I hoped would teach the importance of team unity and ultimately be a tool by which I could get each player to make the commitment of a lifetime.

A friend of mine took a solid piece of oak, four inches by four inches, about two feet long, and had one of his workers cut the piece of solid oak into one hundred pieces. You can imagine the thinness of each piece when you realize that those one hundred pieces once had made up only four inches. I gave a piece of oak to each player, and asked him to hold it carefully because it was fragile. I then picked up one of the four-inch-wide slivers of oak, held it up so the team could see it, and started to bend it just slightly.

It broke, and I said, "It's amazing how weak that piece of oak is when separated from the block." I then asked each player to bring his piece of wood and place it on top of his teammates' pieces until we had all one hundred pieces stacked up.

Then I told them, "Glue and pressure could make that stack of flimsy wood as strong as steel. The bonding of individuals to the purpose of a team, plus the pressure to strive for excellence, can do the same thing for our football team for 1991."

After the meeting, I took the pieces of oak back to my friend, who had his workers glue the pieces together and put them under tremendous pressure until they dried. The next afternoon at our team meeting, I walked in with a solid piece of oak that could not be bent and was as strong as a piece of steel the same size. The players were deeply impressed. I placed the piece of oak on a link of chain, and hung it in the center of their dressing room as a reminder. Phase One of the plan was working.

Phase Two of my plan was put into effect a week prior to our opening game. We'd had good workouts and things were looking pretty positive, but I knew there was one ingredient that we had to have if we were to reach the lofty goals the team members had set for themselves. We had a very tough schedule, and the second game of the season was to be against the defending national champion, the University of Colorado in Boulder. I told our team if we were to reach our goal of being undefeated through the Colorado game it was going to take a strong commitment from every individual player. Each player would have to commit himself to total effort both on and off the football field. Everyone would have to be totally committed to taking care of business, being in class and on time, making all his study sessions, and being at every meeting and practice on time. In other words, they would have to make a total commitment to what it would take in terms of effort.

"And that's not enough to reach our goals," I added. "We must have a commitment to your own physical conditioning—how you take care of your body, abstinence from putting anything in your body that would detract from your ability to contribute one hundred percent to the team. We need a total commitment to the team, to be the best that you can be at your position.

"Finally," I added, "this commitment has to be real. I don't want you just saying that you commit to this because you know that's what I want you to do. It's important that you commit because you want to be a part of the glue that holds this team together in total strength. It must be because you believe in the goals and the purposes of the team. And finally, you must sign your commitment. The four inch by four inch piece of oak must bear your signature of commitment. And I do not want you to sign it until you're totally committed."

It was just prior to the Colorado game before all of the players finally signed the commitment, and as we went to play the University of Colorado on national television, our trainers hung the piece of oak in the center of our visitors' dressing room in Colorado. The piece of oak held the names of all the players and the coaches, who had signed as they made their commitment. That afternoon, Baylor University defeated the University of Colorado, knocking them from the list of the undefeated and beating the defending national champions. In the jubilation of that locker room, the players yelled and shouted and enjoyed their victory, all the while holding above their heads a piece of oak that signified what it had taken for this team to be undefeated and victorious over the defending national champion. The team members had gained strength from each other and created a glue that made the victory happen. Their total commitment to the success of the team had made the difference. Communication and commitment had worked. Little things mean a lot.

Competition is the third seemingly small thing to be considered. Another great American football coach said, "The trouble with American life today, in business as well as in sports, is that too many people are afraid of the competition." Being afraid of competition can stop you in your tracks. Being unafraid of competition can open up new opportunities. In 1982, we signed the number one and number two quarterbacks from the state of Texas: Tom Muecke from Angleton, and Cody Carlson from San Antonio. Both are still playing professional football. Tom is in Canada, and Cody is with the Houston Oilers. It was unusual for any school to try to recruit the two top quarterbacks in the state, but personally I had no hesitation in going after the very best at every position.

It just so happened that both of these young men could play in the system that we were using at Baylor. I knew the competition for both of these guys would be fierce, and it certainly was. I guess my lack of fear in trying to sign them both sent a message that I was a competitor. They could relate to that: Both were great competitors. Later, on the campus, they proved what great competitors they were.

It seemed that the other schools thought that the way to sign either Tom or Cody was to play one against the other, so the two of them were told by many recruiters that the other was definitely going to Baylor. "That means you don't want to go," they would say. "You need to come to our school so you won't have to compete against each other."

What the recruiters were missing was that these two guys hadn't become the best in the state without having a strong competitive spirit, and the other schools were just playing into our hands by trying to convince the players that they shouldn't compete against each other. Both young men were intelligent, and chose to come to Baylor University for other reasons than simply to play football. The day I signed them was one of the happiest days of my life. I knew that we had not only two outstanding athletes, but two individuals of character, intelligence, and tremendous competitiveness.

We had a good quarterback returning the year Tom and Cody were freshman, and I wanted to redshirt both of our new quarterbacks. Cody Carlson got hurt in practice, and he had to redshirt automatically. Tom was not so fortunate, in that just before the TCU game, our quarterback was injured and Tom had to play in the game. It was not an auspicious debut and it cost Tom a year of eligibility, allowing Cody to have one year when Tom was not on campus.

Both guys were baseball players and wanted to play baseball in the spring of their freshman year, but they knew that unless both of them played baseball, one of them would get ahead of the other on the football field. Because both had a chance to start the next year, they elected to participate in spring practice. They were exceptionally equal in talent, and two of the greatest competitors I've ever been around.

At the beginning of the 1983 season, I elected to do what all the critics said could not be done: to have two quarterbacks, alternate them by series, and not choose one over the other. It was not a cop-out on my part. It was just that both of them were so good, and each of them had something unique to contribute to the team. They were always positive and always complimentary about each other, but when they got in a football game, their competitive drive caused each to try and outdo the other whenever he had an opportunity. That, of course, gave us a very strong team and excellent leadership.

In 1985, Tom and Cody led us to the Liberty Bowl with a big victory over Louisiana State University. Cody was selected the Most Valuable Player in that game. The next year, after Tom had graduated, Cody finally had the team by himself, and led us through an outstanding season and to a victory over the University of Colorado in the Bluebonnet Bowl.

A willingness to compete for a position on a team, for a high grade in the classroom, or for a job in the community will ensure eventual success. If either Tom or Cody had been afraid of competition and unwilling to compete against the other, we never could have had the success we had in the 1980s on the football field, and those two young men would not have graduated from the school they really wanted to attend: Baylor University. Little things mean a lot.

14.
Do the Best You Can with What You Have

David, the young man who had made a commitment to fight the giant Goliath for his nation, was given the opportunity to do so by the leader of that nation. But the king wanted David to wear a specially made helmet, to put heavy armor around himself, and to use a sword that had been made for the king. David politely refused to wear the helmet, use the armor, or wield the sword. He could not be somebody else; he had to use his own talent and ability the best way he knew how. David said, "I have to be who I am, and do it my way."

This was a very intelligent move on the young man's part. First of all, he was not trained in the skills of a warrior, and the helmet, armor, and sword would merely have weighed him down. On the other hand, he was skilled in the art of using a sling, a device made of a large piece of leather with a long strap tied on either end. The piece of leather was large enough to hold a stone that could be twirled over the head, building up velocity. Then one of the straps could be turned loose at exactly the right time and the stone would be hurled with great speed at the target.

Prior to his encounter with Goliath, David's targets had been the wild animals that had tried to devour his father's sheep. This time, the target was Goliath, who was probably twice as tall as David, and outweighed him by several hundred pounds. But the principle worked then and applies just as strongly today.

Too many people want what someone else has. They sit around saying, "I wish I could be that person's size, or have that person's intelligence or financial resources," instead of looking at their own talents and abilities and resources, and using them to the fullest.

It's important to remember that not only is there a time and place for everything, but there's a spot on the team for everyone. However, not everyone can play the same position. Gerald McNeil is an example of this. Gerald was from Killeen, Texas. The day I signed him, he weighed 138 pounds. He was close to 5'6", and in the four years he spent at Baylor he didn't grow very much. What was interesting was that Gerald McNeil had been a defensive back in high school and a darn good one, but I felt he had the ability to become a wide receiver. Even though he was very short, he was very fast. He also had a lot of physical toughness. That was really one of the reasons we offered him a scholarship. So it was a surprise when the Baylor team doctors examined Gerald and discovered he had been playing football all those years with what seemed to be a serious spinal problem. It looked for a while as though his career might end before it started. But then our trainer took Gerald to Houston to a specialist, who said that although Gerald's spine was out of alignment and had been that way since childhood, he could still play football in college. He did, and never had a problem with his back.

The thing that was so impressive about Gerald was that he used every ounce of talent he had. Gerald had excellent hand-eye coordination, ran his routes precisely, and had tremendous speed once he caught the ball. In spite of this, he had the skill and talent to play only one position out of twenty-two on a college football team. He used that talent to become Baylor's leading receiver and to go on after graduation to a distinguished career in the NFL. He did it his way, not someone else's.

So the basics for this principle are: First, discover and develop your own skills, talents, and abilities. Second, be who you are, not somebody else. No one is born perfect, so there's always something you will not like about yourself, or something you do not have that you admire in somebody else. Don't waste your time wishing for what someone else has; rather, spend your time developing what you have. Do the best you can with what *you* have.

> *"We help our bilingual students realize that even though they cannot speak English, they have other accomplishments," said Joyce. "We try to help them understand that, while they are learning English, it is better for them if they keep their Spanish (or other language) because speaking two languages is an advantage. We want them to be the best they can be as bilingual students."*

15.
Overcoming Criticism

Donald T. Phillips, in *Lincoln on Leadership*, quotes Abraham Lincoln as saying, "I do the very best I know how, the very best I can, and I mean to keep on doing it until the very end. If the end brings me out all right, what is said against me will not amount to anything. If the end brings me out wrong, ten legions of angels swearing I was right would make no difference."

I used to tell my players that there will always be those around you who will try to put you down and fill you with negative thoughts about yourself. Don't listen. Believe in yourself and believe you're going to be successful. The critics always will be there ready to seize any opportunity to criticize. But you can turn that to your own advantage. For example, if someone tells me I can't do something, it's like pouring gasoline on a smoldering ember: It lights me up. I love the challenge of someone saying it can't be done.

When I took the Baylor job in 1972, it had been turned down by scores of coaches, both head coaches and assistants. Although I had been a head coach for nine years (six at McMurry College and three at Angelo State) the critics really didn't think Knute Rockne could win at

Baylor, much less Grant Teaff from Angelo State. Right after I accepted the job, a Dallas newspaper ran a bold headline that said: "Henceforth, Baylor Stadium will be known as Grant's Tomb." Other newspapers simply asked, "Grant Who?"

Now a coach who can't take criticism is in the wrong business. However, I freely admit that, being a very sensitive person, I found the criticism sometimes stung, but I didn't let on. I knew that I knew what I was doing, and that I could be successful where few other people could be successful, and that if someone didn't understand why I was doing something and wanted to criticize me for it, it was okay.

There was one piece of criticism that I thoroughly enjoyed turning the tables on, however. In the late eighties there was an offensive football strategy by the name of "run and shoot." This strategy virtually eliminated the run in football and relied almost totally on the passing game. The statistics to back up its use were truly outstanding. But in 1990, I consciously moved Baylor's offensive strategy back to the option running game at a time when the media thought everyone should be moving toward the run and shoot. Amid heavy criticism, I stuck to my guns.

In 1991 and 1992 we soundly defeated the University of Houston, with, of all things, a controlled running game. Without being smug and saying I told you so, I had an advantage. I knew our system had worked over a long period of time. I knew that we had a strong defense based on the fact that our own defense had to play against our physical running offensive philosophy. The run-and-shoot defense, I believed, would deteriorate over a period of time, because in spring practice and early season work, the defensive team could not get the proper training while playing against their own offense. The important thing was that I believed in what I was doing, so I ignored the criticism, and like Abraham Lincoln said, it was okay because it came out right on the other end.

Others I've known who endured and overcame criticism include Baylor University's 1974 starting quarterback, senior Neal Jeffrey, who, you might remember, was a stutterer. In his junior year, Neal had handled criticism very well when he had mistakenly thrown the ball out of bounds to stop the clock. The only problem with that was that it was fourth down, and Baylor lost the game. I was impressed with his handling of the criticism that came his way then, but the way he handled an incident in Fayetteville, Arkansas, was even more impressive.

On the Friday afternoon before our game against the University of Arkansas Razorbacks, we arrived in Rogers, a few miles north of Fayetteville, where we were staying for the night. We had practiced, eaten our evening meal, and now all of us, players and coaches, were sitting around the pool just visiting. The afternoon Arkansas papers had arrived, and almost everybody, including Neal, was reading about the game.

One of the players came up to me and said, "Coach, have you seen this article about Neal?"

I said, "No. I haven't seen the paper."

He said, "You need to read this. I think it's really going to bother Neal."

The writer had likened Neal to a general in charge of an army. The general stuttered, and when his army was marching toward a cliff and he realized what his soldiers were doing, he started trying to say, "Halt!" Because of his speech problem, the army marched off the cliff to their destruction. That, the sportswriter said, was the way it would be the next day when the Baylor Bears went off the cliff because their stuttering quarterback was unable to stop them.

After reading the article, I called Neal aside, wanting to say some encouraging words.

I asked him, "Have you read the article?"

He said, "Yeah, I just finished reading it."

"How did it make you feel?" I asked him.

"Well, it hurt my feelings and embarrassed me a little bit, but if the writer intended for it to bother me, it really didn't."

Neal went into the game the next day without letting the writer's words discourage him, and he was responsible for the team's upset victory over Arkansas, 21-17. (Later, the sportswriter who had written the article was declared persona non grata by Baylor University. He was not welcome in Baylor Stadium, or on Baylor campus.)

Another example of people who've overcome criticism is Derek Turner, who came to Baylor as a walk-on from the state of Oklahoma. He was from a small school, and he was dyslexic. All he wanted was a chance to play and earn an education. He'd been told by a lot of people throughout his life that he wasn't good enough to play college football, and he wasn't smart enough to get an education. Derek Turner never listened to the criticism, and would not let it keep him from achieving his goals. While at Baylor, he earned a scholarship, became an all-Conference defensive end, and won the SWC's highest award, the American Spirit Award, which is given to the outstanding scholar/athlete/player combined. He was fortunate in having great support from his parents, and later from his wife, whom he met at Baylor. Today, Derek is a very successful businessman in Oklahoma. He would be quick to tell you that overcoming adversity is a lot easier when you have strong support from those you love.

> *"We help our students overcome the criticism that always accompanies a bilingual program by teaching them to have great pride in themselves and in the program," said Joyce.*

"Many of our critics think that the children should have to learn their academic subjects in English right from the time they enroll, and so we have to prove that our program is useful. Our purpose is to teach the students English, but also to keep up their academic progress. We tell students to prove those who criticize bilingual programs wrong. This approach seems to work pretty well."

"Strangely enough," said Bob, "the success I have so far had with helping kids view criticism as an incentive to do better has been with the math program I recently set up on the computers. It prints out a critique of the students' performance at the end of each set of problems, telling them how many problem were done correctly and incorrectly. Then it tells them, 'You should ask for the More Hints section of the program, and you should do over again the problems that you missed.' The students read the critiques really carefully. They love to keep what the computer says about them. If I said the same thing, the students would question me or take my suggestion that they redo it amiss, but if they read it from a computer printout, they can take the assessment as it is meant to be taken."

16.
Being Tenacious

Tenacity can be described this way, "Believing in yourself and never entertaining the thought of giving up or being unsuccessful." The ability to stick with it, to persevere, to never quit will put you in a position to be successful. I've seen it happen over and over again. In 1993, for example, J. J. Joe became the all-time passer for Baylor University, but that wasn't the way it started out.

In the spring of J. J. Joe's freshman year, he ended up the fourth-team quarterback. I personally had had high aspirations for J. J. He was an outstanding student with great football savvy, and a very good arm. However, in practice and in scrimmages, J. J. looked as if he did not know one end of the football from the other. At the end of spring practice, the football staff's evaluation of J. J. was extremely critical. He had shown no leadership, they said, had demonstrated poor ball handling, and had not thrown the ball with any effectiveness. They projected that he would remain the fourth-team quarterback and spend probably another year as a redshirt, participating on the scout team.

But when the team reported in August of 1990, our coaching staff was surprised to see how finely conditioned

J. J. was. He led all the quarterbacks, running backs, and wide receivers in the conditioning test. I was as surprised as anyone else. Having been around J. J. for only a year, I didn't fully understand his tenacity. Nor did I realize that he was not happy with being the fourth-team quarterback and had no intention of spending another year on the scout team. Nonetheless, even though he had good practices in August, he was still not ready to play when we started the season against Nebraska. Then Brad Goebel, our starting quarterback for three years, hurt a knee and was unable to play against the University of Nebraska. So Steve Needham, the backup quarterback, started the game.

Two weeks later, on the Thursday before an open date, our team experienced a terrible tragedy: the death of a teammate. There was a lot of emotion, a funeral and memorial service, and no preparation for the Saturday game in Lubbock against Texas Tech University. Brad Goebel had recovered from his knee injury and started the game against Texas Tech, but we were unable to move the ball. Somehow our defense kept us in the game, and then, midway through the second quarter, Brad broke his hand. J. J. was as prepared as any backup quarterback we had, so he was put in the game and led the Baylor Bears to a come-from-behind victory against Texas Tech.

With the exception of a couple of times when he was injured, for the rest of that season and the next three years, J. J. was our starting quarterback. He led Baylor to many victories, one of the greatest being over the University of Arizona in the John Hancock Bowl in December 1992.

Abe Lincoln was one of the greatest failures of all time. He failed in business, he could not win an election, and it looked as though his life might end in hopeless failure. But, because he was tenacious and continued to run for public office, he became the savior of our nation. In some ways he was like the great heavyweight champion,

Rocky Marciano. When Rocky was asked how he became the heavyweight champion of the world, he said, "By fighting one more round." Abe Lincoln kept on until he got it right. Just one more election, and he became the President of the United States of America.

"Encouraging my students to persevere includes telling them about people they know who've been successful in difficult circumstances," said Don. "I also tell them my story. I didn't go to university in four years, I went at night for ten years. It wasn't easy, and I faced a lot of adversity, but I got it done. I think it works much better if the kids can know the person who's overcome difficulties. Because of this, I bring former students back in who've got good jobs. They'll tell my students that they used to get into trouble, or that they had obstacles to overcome, but they stuck with it, graduated, and got a good job. The kids really respond."

"I encourage the children to keep trying by telling them stories about my personal life, or about people I know who have overcome failure or difficulties and still made it. We also get our students involved in programs that help migrant and bilingual students with funding and tutoring," said Joyce. "We try to raise money for them and to help them acquire the prerequisites for college, or have the college waive those requirements for some students. We also provide help for others who are not going to college. We bring back our graduated students to encourage the current students to stay

in school. We have monthly parent teacher meetings to encourage parents to help their kids stay in school. This is often hard with migrant families, especially in regard to their girls."

17.
Being Courageous

Ralph Waldo Emerson said, "Whatever you do, you need courage. Whatever course you decide upon, there is always someone to tell you that you are wrong. There are always difficulties arising which tempt you to believe that your critics are right. To map out a course of action and follow it to an end requires some of the same courage which a soldier needs. Peace has its victories, but it takes a brave man to win them."

Socrates said, "Courage is knowing what not to fear." Courage can translate into doing an unreasonable act for good reasons. But courage is more than that. It's also knowing that courage alone will not suffice: To successfully carry out something that requires courage, you must have acquired the knowledge and developed the skills to succeed.

Courage is not the accepting of a dare to do something you shouldn't do. If you accepted a dare to join the famous Wallenda family of high-flying aerialists in a death-defying walk between two of the highest buildings in the world, you might be called "courageous"; yet if you don't have the knowledge and the developed skills, you should more properly be called "suicidal."

Confucius said, "To see what is right, and not do it, is want of courage." It takes courage to do the right thing, so a life without courage is miserable. It takes courage to find a purpose in all that you do, to cultivate successful habits, to develop fully the little things that make the difference. It takes courage to recognize that you must use the talent you have to the best of your ability. It takes great courage to overcome criticism, and courage to be tenacious in all that you do. Courage is not merely avoiding danger, it's conquering it. Courage means that you recognize that you have to be smarter than the equipment you're using. Courage is doing a job it's easier not to do. Courage is making the right decision.

As human beings we have the right to choose. We have a brain that allows us to feed in information that hopefully will let us make the proper decisions. But it takes real courage to understand that our everyday decisions affect the outcome of our lives. It takes courage to read, watch, and listen to individuals and subject matter that will allow us to succeed. It takes courage to choose not to ride with someone who's been drinking. It takes tremendous courage to choose not to associate with individuals whose thoughts and actions could keep us from reaching our goals.

This was highlighted by an incident in the life of Dr. David Livingstone, the famous missionary to Africa. A group trying to assist him wrote him a letter that asked: "Have you found a good road to where you are? If so, we want to know how to send other men to you." Livingstone's reply came: "If you have men who will come only if they know there's a good road, I don't want them. I want men strong and courageous who will come if there is no road at all."

We live in a society where courageous men and women have blazed new trails in science, medicine, and space. We have one of the highest living standards of any nation in the world, yet we have many problems still facing us. Someone will have to develop the knowledge, skills, and techniques to step forward and courageously solve the problems that we face today. That person will make a difference. As Andrew Jackson said, "One man with courage makes a majority."

During the 1960 Olympic Games in Rome, Italy, a young woman from Clarksville, Tennessee, made history. She became the first U.S. woman to win three gold medals in track and field. Her name is Wilma Rudolph, and not only was she the world's greatest woman sprinter, but she was also one of the best basketball players ever to play the game. While starring at Tennessee State University, she received a degree so that she might become a teacher and help other young people.

Wilma Rudolph's great accomplishments in 1960 were the culmination of the attitude that characterized her: *I can*. To understand just how far this young lady had come to achieve those accomplishments, you have to go back to the day of her birth. She was a four and one-half pound baby, not a good birth weight in those days. In fact, at the time of her birth, her parents, Ed and Blanche Rudolph, wondered if their new daughter would live, much less be able to run.

The child lived, but her problems were not over. At age four, she contracted double pneumonia and scarlet fever at the same time. With the support of a loving family and a mother who spent endless hours taking her to Nashville for weekly heat therapy and leg massages, Wilma began to improve. By the time she was eight years old, she was able to walk with the aid of a specially constructed shoe. At age eleven, she started to play basketball, and by the time she reached high school, she had blossomed into an all-State girls basketball player.

Then Wilma was given a scholarship to Tennessee State University, and never lost a race in three seasons. At the Olympics, she won against the best in the world. Wilma Rudolph is now a teacher and a lecturer, a mother, and an inspiration to all of us. It took courage for Wilma Rudolph to go through those years of painful rehabilitation. It took courage for her family to spend hours helping her overcome her physical problems.

It takes courage to seize the opportunities that are available.

> *"I love to use the example of Les Brown,"* said Wade. *"He's a guy from Atlanta who was declared functionally illiterate in high school. But he's been a congressman, and is a great motivational speaker. I've met him and have introduced his motivational tapes to my students. Sticking it out the way Les Brown did is a real example of courage."*

18.
Having Great Expectations

The highest level of performance takes place within the framework of expectation. As an athlete I never played in a game I didn't expect to win. As a coach, I never coached a game I didn't expect to win. Arrogance, you say? Far from it. As an athlete I was not the biggest, strongest, or fastest, and I knew it. But in my own mind I was the most well-prepared guy on the field, from a physical and a technical standpoint, and because I had the right winning attitude. Those conditions were self-imposed.

In my coaching profession, career decisions always put me with programs that were unsuccessful, that had many problems and great challenges. As I look back, I seem to thrive on that combination. Accomplishing what others think cannot be accomplished, sometimes winning with individuals nobody else wants, is satisfying and rewarding to me. In each instance, be it in a school or a game, or with an individual, there was in my mind the confident expectation of success:

- I went to San Angelo College as a 17-year-old freshman without a scholarship. I expected to earn one, and I did.

- As a walk-on at San Angelo College, I expected to start every game, and I did.
- After two years of junior college, I expected to receive a scholarship at a four-year institution, and I did.
- At McMurry College I expected to be the captain of the team, to start every game on offense and defense, and I did.
- I expected to finish my education at McMurry College with an undergraduate degree and a master's degree, and I did.
- I expected to be a college coach. After one year of coaching at a high school, I became the head track coach and the assistant football coach at McMurry College.
- Though I had no experience as a track coach, I expected to have the best small-college track team in Texas, and one of the best in America. I did.
- I expected to be the head football coach as well as the head track coach at McMurry College. When the head football coach left McMurry, I was promoted and held both positions.
- McMurry College gave up all its scholarships. I expected to reinstate those scholarships and get McMurry to join the Lone Star Conference. I did.
- I expected to get an offer to coach on a Division 1A level. J. T. King provided that offer at Texas Tech.
- Texas Tech had never beaten the University of Texas. As an assistant coach at Tech, I expected to beat Texas. We did.
- Angelo State University had never had a winning season as a four-year institution. I expected to win the very first year, and we did.

- Baylor University's football program was on the brink of extinction, having not had a winning season in many years and winning only three games in the previous three years. I expected to win, and we did.

Throughout my coaching career, confidence in my own ability and in that of my coaching staff helped create a positive expectation for success. A good work ethic, a positive attitude, the daily use of goals, and the application of the sound principles of success were the foundation for that positive expectation.

> *"Positive expectations are really important," said Don. "In one class I teach, called Computer Integrated Manufacturing, the kids turn expectations into products. They get in small groups and form their own companies. I don't even know in what direction they're going to go, but I always expect the best out of them, and they deliver it. They make up a company name, design a logo, come up with an idea, and from that idea they have to make a sketch, then a CAD drawing to get a blueprint. Then they actually manufacture the part. Of course, they've already learned the principles that allow them to do this, but I think it's equally important that they know I expect them to be able to deliver."*

It needs to be noted that just because you always expect to succeed doesn't mean that you always will. In a football game, half the teams lose unless there is a tie. In life, you may come up against someone who has equally high expectations and is better prepared. This was my case in the second grade, when the "I can do attitude" that has always marked me got me in serious trouble.

Lowell Bynum and I had been neighbors and friends since we were toddlers. Lowell, who later became a very successful band director and professor of music on the college level, was obviously musically inclined. I certainly was not. (I've described my musical talent as being less than able to play the radio.) Totally tone deaf and without one ounce of preparation, I let my positive expectations run away with me one morning in second grade.

Our elementary school was attached to the junior high, and that was attached to the high school in Snyder, Texas. One Tuesday, a couple of seniors from the high school walked into our classroom and explained that on the coming Friday, there would be a talent show with participants from the elementary, junior high, and high schools. Just the day before, our second-grade teacher had unpacked and passed out the musical instruments that we had ordered so that we could form a tonette band. (A tonette is a flute-like instrument, about 8-10" long, and by blowing into the instrument and putting your fingers on the proper holes, you can create the most beautiful melodies.) Our teacher had earlier demonstrated the tonette, and we had all enthusiastically decided to learn to play the instrument.

When the high-school students asked for volunteers, Lowell Bynum's hand went up. Little did I know that Lowell already knew how to play the tonette, and so when he enthusiastically said he would play his tonette in the talent show on Friday, my little hand went up instantaneously. When the seniors' eyes fell on me, I said, "I'll play the tonette, too." Some sheet music happened to be lying on top of the desk when I was asked for my selection. My eyes fell on the title of the sheet music and I said, "I will play *Twinkle, Twinkle Little Star.*"

My classmates were tremendously impressed. I'm sure my teacher was stunned. And for some reason, Lowell Bynum had a smug little smile on his face.

Somehow, without one moment's training, I expected to walk on that stage and have the melodious tones of *Twinkle, Twinkle Little Star* float out through the audience. Naturally, I expected a standing ovation when I finished my piece. However, it didn't work out exactly the way I expected. That Friday, when my name was called, I walked out onto the stage. There was no place for my sheet music, which I could not read anyway, so I laid it on the stage in front of me. The students started to laugh. I guess they thought it was part of a comedy routine. I spread my legs over the sheet music, looked down, placed the tonette into my mouth, and started to play.

Much to my chagrin, *Twinkle, Twinkle Little Star* never came out. Instead, what I produced was the most goshawful sound that you've ever heard. The harder I blew, the more terrible the sound. As the laughter reached a crescendo, I ran off the stage and up the aisle to my teacher. Then I proceeded to jump into her lap and cry uncontrollably.

It was a terrible experience, but somehow I survived it and learned a great lesson about expectations. Great expectations alone will not allow you to be successful. Preparation, knowledge, and sheer determination are essential parts of the framework that allows the confidence of great expectations to give you victory and success.

"I agree that great expectations alone are not enough for success. Sometimes, students in my Computer Integrated Manufacturing class tell me, 'We're going to make this product out of steel,' and I have to tell them, 'Steel is too heavy for that part. You'll have to

> *think of something else,'" said Don. "Then they*
> *decide on another material and figure out how*
> *they'll have to manufacture the part. They have*
> *the framework of knowledge, but they have to*
> *learn to adapt to the situation they are in.*
> *When they use the knowledge they've acquired*
> *to figure out a substitute material, then they*
> *can build the product successfully."*

Expecting to win is a mind-set, an attitude that has to be developed. There's a cord that runs through all achievers, no matter what their field of endeavor. That cord is made up of six strands, all beginning with the letter "P." They form the Six Ps of Great Expectations: possibilities, planning, preparation, practice, patience, and perseverance.

Possibilities: Each opportunity in life must be looked at as a possibility for success.

Planning: Planning takes time and effort, wise counsel and good decisions, and always includes goal-setting. One of the first goals that you should set is to be successful in what you're planning, because planning is only as good as the preparation that goes into it.

Preparation: Taking the aspects of the plan that cannot be practiced, make sure that every detail is prepared. For instance, in football when you're playing on artificial turf, there's a great difference between wet turf and dry turf. All your preparation for victory and all your great expectations can be wiped out if you do not have the proper footwear for your team: gripper cleats if it ends up raining, flat soles if it's a dry field. While this factor goes unnoticed by the fans watching the game, it is imperative to victory.

Practice: The execution and practice of planning are essential. The old adage says "practice makes perfect."

You may not always have enough time to become perfect, but you always have sufficient time to practice enough so that you can execute the plans properly. When you do, you'll feel that surge of confidence that goes with planning, preparation, and practice.

Patience: Those who want to reach their great expectations must have patience. We've all seen individuals and teams go into a contest or event with great expectations and the confidence to win. But the moment something bad happens, they show a tendency to panic and lose concentration. Patience is essential to achieving those great expectations, because it allows you to recognize and understand that not everything will go well in your efforts. Bad things *are* going to happen; you just have to wait them out. Stay with your plan. Continue to believe that you're going to be successful, and ultimately, find a way to reach what you believed you could reach.

Perseverance: Simply described, perseverance is hanging in there, believing you're going to win, doing to the very last minute whatever it takes to be successful. Amazingly, most of the time, you *will* be successful. For example, after winning the 1993 Super Bowl, the Dallas Cowboys began the 1994 season by losing thoroughly. As the media began to write off the Cowboys' chance for the 1994 Super Bowl, observers noticed that Coach Jimmy Johnson kept saying that his team's goal was to *win* the 1994 Super Bowl—not simply to *get in* the Super Bowl, but to *win.*

When the Cowboys moved into the playoffs, their next opponent was the San Francisco 49ers, who had dominated professional football in the eighties. Part of Coach Jimmy Johnson's strength as a coach is the fact that he expects to win. Like all good coaches, he doesn't always make that fact known, because he is a good user of psychology. He knows that while you may be confident and believe you're going to win, you don't throw that in the face of an opponent at just any time. There are appropriate times for such an action.

Such a time came on a radio talk show early in the week prior to the San Francisco game, when Coach Johnson stated very clearly and unequivocally, "We *will* win the game." He expected to win, he knew that his team expected to win, and psychologically, it was the right time to let the San Francisco 49ers, his home team, and everyone else know that, beyond a shadow of a doubt, he believed they were going to win. They did win, and went on to win their second Super Bowl.

The media asked, "Did the Cowboys win because Jimmy Johnson said they were going to win?" I don't think so. I think the Cowboys won for the same reason you can win: They applied the six Ps.

When I first went to Baylor in December of 1972, everyone expected Baylor to lose any football game against the University of Texas. It had been sixteen years since Baylor had had a victory against Texas, and "dominance" was the word thrown around by sportswriters concerning Texas's role in the series between Texas and Baylor. When I was at Texas Tech, I had found a similar attitude. The Texas Tech Red Raiders had never beaten the University of Texas, and there was the prevailing attitude that they just couldn't beat Texas. With no background to support that negative feeling, I was able to look at Texas very analytically. After seeing a game in person and looking at film, I thought Texas Tech *could* win against the University of Texas and so I proceeded to tell the coaching staff and the players. At a Monday Red Raider club meeting in downtown Lubbock, J. T. King, the head coach at Texas Tech, asked me to tell the members about the Texas team we were about to play. When I concluded talking about the strengths and weaknesses of the University of Texas, I just said flat out, "We *will* beat the University of Texas." I don't think Coach King was very happy with me for saying that, but on our way back to the stadium, he accepted the fact that I really believed it, and expected to win. Of course, it didn't really matter if *I* believed it: The key was whether the Texas Tech football team believed it and could go into the game with an expectation to win.

The players developed that expectancy to win through their use of the coaching staff's "six Ps," and we beat the University of Texas in Austin. Coming back from Austin, our plane could not land at the Lubbock airport because of the cheering crowds out on the runway. The next year, our players at Texas Tech *expected* to win against Texas, and we did. So, when I came to Baylor, I came with a confidence that few Baylor people had, in that I'd been involved in beating the University of Texas while an assistant at Texas Tech, and after looking at and evaluating the University of Texas offense, I believed sincerely that Baylor could win. This was in spite of the fact that, by the time Baylor played the University of Texas in 1974, Texas already had won six SWC championships, and was well on their way to their seventh.

The 1974 game was to be played in Waco. A large crowd was there to witness the game, and, as usual, I really expected to defeat Texas that day. However, by half-time my expectancy had dwindled. We were down 24-7 and Texas was dominating our team. Going up our tunnel to the dressing room, I looked to my left and saw I was walking beside our quarterback, Neal Jeffrey. Being down 24-7, with Baylor having lost to Texas eighteen straight times prior to this, I fully expected to see him with a long sad face and a faraway look. Instead, what I saw and heard made my heart beat faster. Neal looked me right in the eye, and said, "Coach, we're going to win this football game."

Before I could ask why, he told me.

"We've been able to move the ball. They've had some big breaks on their offense. They're going to be

161

overconfident. We've got 'em right where we want 'em, Coach."

I just smiled at the power of positive expectation, because now Neal had me feeling again like we could win. We went into the dressing room and he talked to every player in the room individually, telling them that we were going to go out and win the football game. We did, and went on to win the first SWC championship in fifty years.

Oh, the power of positive expectations.

19.
Turning a Setback into a Comeback

The true measure of a winner is how he handles defeat. Anyone can handle a victory, but when it comes to overcoming a defeat, it takes a special person with a special attitude. Every human being suffers defeat, though many think it never will happen to them. Since this is sometimes true of very successful coaches, when I'm speaking to a group of coaches at a clinic, I usually say to them, "I'd like to meet everyone who has never tasted the bitter taste of defeat, immediately following the program." Then I tell them, "I have some bad news for you. Defeat is right around the corner. It's gonna hit you right in the face. It's gonna knock you flat on your back. You're gonna be looking up at the stars and saying, 'Why me?' Defeat comes to everyone. How will *you* handle defeat?"

All defeats hurt, whether they're large or small. But some defeats have a more lasting effect on us than others. It hurts to fail a test or miss a tackle or lose a game, but the loss of a friend or an opportunity is a stinging, bitter defeat in many ways. One of the most remarkable examples I could give concerning overcoming a terrible defeat began in 1979. That year, Kyle Woods was a red-shirt sophomore on the Baylor team. In early August, he went in to make a tackle, broke his neck, and became a quadriplegic, paralyzed from the neck down.

Most of us never will understand the pain and humiliation that Kyle Woods went through. The loss of mobility and the loss of opportunity are sometimes overwhelming for me to think about even now. But Kyle is a remarkable young man. Some time after he was injured, having lost 60 pounds, he went into rehabilitation and became an inspiration to literally hundreds of people. Our football team was so moved by Kyle's attitude and ability to bounce back from such a tragic defeat, that in that same 1979 season, the team pledged to beat Clemson University in the Peach Bowl to honor Kyle. And they did.

Then, in early November 1980, Kyle Woods came back to Baylor for the homecoming game against the University of Arkansas. It had been a year and three months since the night he had been injured, and in that time he had not been back to Baylor Stadium. The homecoming game that Kyle was to attend was a very important one, since the Bears were undefeated in Conference play, with an opportunity to go on and win the SWC. Despite this, the team was not in good psychological shape. The week before, Baylor had been knocked from the undefeated list in college football by a stunning loss to San Jose State. San Jose State had a good football team, but they were not supposed to beat Baylor. So the week prior to the Arkansas game had been one of almost doom and gloom. The chance for a national championship had been lost and now the team had to bounce back from that and go on and win a Conference championship. That was easier said than done.

The Arkansas game was to be on television, but I knew we were not ready for prime time because mentally we were still more concerned about the loss we had experienced than about the chance to win the SWC championship. More thought was being given to the game that had been lost, than to the upcoming game. If we won against Arkansas, we would have a chance to be the conference champions, but for some reason the black cloud of "Oh, what might have been," hung heavily over our team. I didn't know what I could say that would change that.

In the dressing room prior to the ball game, Kyle was smiling as he greeted all of his teammates. Sitting upright in his wheelchair, he waited for the team to go out on the field to begin the game. I was grasping for something to say to them when I suddenly realized that Kyle was in the room, and it was his first time back at Baylor Stadium. It was symbolic: We were about to play a homecoming game, one that was important to all of us, and here was Kyle, "home" for the first time since his accident. So I turned to him and said, "Kyle, do you have anything to say to this team?" He smiled and nodded his head in affirmation. I walked over behind him and pushed the wheelchair to the center of the room, which was filled with coaches and players, trainers and managers. Starting on the right side of the room and slowly turning his head all the way to the left, Kyle seemingly looked every individual in the eye. You could have heard a pin drop.

Then he said, "Here it is. You have to take a setback and turn it into a comeback."

As everyone's eyes widened and they began to think about what Kyle had said, I saw him straighten his back. His hands dropped down on the edge of the wheelchair, he arched his back, and somehow lunged forward, rocked up on his feet, and stood up in the room to punctuate what he had just said. Mike Liveley was standing close by and he reached out to steady Kyle as he stood in the room.

What a moment!

You could take all the losses that Baylor University had ever had in the history of the school and put them in a pile, and they would be insignificant compared to the loss that Kyle had suffered. And here, to emphasize his point, somehow, someway, for the first time and for the last time, Kyle stood in that room.

Of course, Arkansas didn't have a chance that day. Baylor won handily. Every player, every coach, and everyone who had heard the words of Kyle Woods knew where the inspiration had come from. The loss and the setback that had deterred the team from mentally being ready to play were challenged by the simple statement, "Take a setback and turn it into a comeback."

> *"I think to help students turn setbacks into comebacks, you have to always be encouraging," said Don. "I often tell my students, 'Keep trying. I'm going to keep plugging away with you, to try and help you become a better person, as long as you keep coming to my class.' Some of them respond well to that, and some—well, they never see it. But you can't give up."*

IV.
Keys to Motivation

I don't believe that success is a matter of luck. I think it's a matter of work, work, and work. None of the principles, characteristics, and habits of success can bear fruit until hard work, properly directed, occurs.

—Grant Teaff

I teach in an inner-city area, and I see young bright kids filled with dreams . . . who never actually practice or plan or get enthusiastic. So they don't achieve their dreams.

—Bob Roth, high-school teacher
Dexter, Michigan

INTRODUCTION
Types of Motivation

Motivation is that which propels you into action and maintains your action. Translated, that means that a drive or a desire is created within you to accomplish, and then to continue to accomplish. Creating motivation is one thing, sustaining motivation is another.

Here's a scenario: A young boy becomes very impressed with two high-school coaches. He wants to be just like them, teaching others the game of football and how to be successful. Although he is small and slow, he wants very much to please his family and his coaches and learn the game. However, he realizes that in order to coach and teach he has to get a college degree. To get a college degree, he has to find the money to pay for the education. One way this young man could pay for his education is by earning a scholarship with his football ability. But remember now, this young man is small and slow. These are not the basic criteria for earning a college football scholarship. The young man is not offered a scholarship, but, to reach his goals, he decides to try out with a junior-college team that offers the opportunity to earn a scholarship. The young man earns a scholarship, then goes on to get a college degree and to reach his goals of becoming a coach.

What caused the young man to achieve success? The answer is motivation. A desire was created in the young boy to emulate two people he admired. The successful completion of high school and his finding a way to get a degree built on his original motivation, creating in the young man a further deep desire to reach his goals and forcing him to find within himself ways to do that. The action was started by motivation and sustained by motivation.

That young man was, of course, Grant Teaff, and that first experience of recognizing a desire began to unlock for me the world of motivation. Being conscious of an inner drive created by a desire, I learned that there are other motivational forces. One is fear motivation, which is created by threat, a concern for reprisal, or the fear of failure. I've talked to many successful individuals, and when I asked them to define the motivation behind their success, many said, "The fear of failure motivated me to work harder than anything else. I was afraid I would fail."

If you're concerned about what someone else thinks, or about the end results of your actions, you're motivated by fear—fear of failure. When you're told that a set of penalties will be invoked if you do not behave to a certain standard, then fear of the penalties motivates you to behave in a certain manner.

I was fortunate enough to live in a small town where I could get a job when I was ten years old, working in a grocery store. Because I worked all week, on Saturday nights my parents allowed me to walk about three blocks to the main square after I'd finished my job. There I'd go to see a movie with some of my friends. One particular night, we saw a movie that used the power of fear to entertain the audience. Though we laughed about the scary show, when we left the movie we were all a little scared. We went in separate directions to our homes, and I had to walk only about five blocks to mine. To get there, however, I had to

170

walk through some big cottonwood trees just off the square where there were no street lights. I *had* to walk through them. The wind was blowing so the limbs of the trees were moving and the leaves were making a strange noise as they rubbed together. I believe if I had been clocked that night on a one-hundred-yard dash, I might have been close to a world record. I know that neither before nor since have I ever run that fast. I wanted to get past those trees and get in my house where my mother and dad were, and I ran fast because I was afraid. I was motivated by fear.

Another form of motivation is incentive motivation. We've all seen the picture of the donkey pulling a cart, loaded and heavy. The donkey has a pole attached to the harness that extends out about two feet in front of his head. Attached to the end of the pole on a string dangles a juicy carrot. As the donkey steps toward the carrot, he pulls the cart. He never gets to the carrot, but he continues to pull the cart step after step. Cruel, you say, but not so different from other forms of incentive motivation to which we all respond: Salesmen who reach a certain sales goal will receive a bonus. Individuals who work for large companies often get to take trips in the summer as a bonus for accomplishing certain goals within their jobs. Pay incentives have long driven the business world. The harder you work, the more you achieve, the more money you can make. A lot of young athletes in our society today look up to professional athletes, who become role models because of their salaries and lifestyles. Thus the motivational incentive is to achieve the financial status of a professional athlete. Every college basketball player wants to be in the Final Four and to wear the championship ring. Bowl games are the incentive for college football players. To get to go to a Bowl and enjoy the entertainment, to receive the free gifts that come for participation in a Bowl, as well as to enjoy the opportunity to play on television, are all forms of incentive.

"In some classes," said Joyce, "I find I have to keep changing techniques to give the students something new to motivate them. The kids, mostly ninth and tenth graders, are always interested in math, but with language arts, they have a lot of trouble. Part of that may be cultural, since not too much value is placed on language-arts skills in their culture."

"Because of the lack of motivation in the classroom," said Wade, "we teachers are having to learn to be entertainers and motivators."

20.
Self-Motivation

I have experienced all the different types of motivation and have used them at one time or another in my life. However, I'm firmly convinced that the truest form of motivation, the most lasting form of motivation, and the best form of motivation, is self-motivation.

Gas-powered engines will not move until they are ignited with an electrical charge. In older engines there was a button that could be pushed to allow the electrical charge to start the engine. Because the result of pushing that button was a running engine, it was said that in order to get your engine running, you had to push your "hot button."

Self-motivation, then, is finding your own hot button, pushing it at the appropriate time, and thus propelling yourself into action. To find your hot button, you must master some basic techniques. Self-evaluation, recognizing your strengths and weaknesses, learning what talents and abilities you possess, and learning to master those talents and abilities are all necessary.

Step One to Self-Motivation: Evaluation

Take a piece of paper. On the top left side of the paper write the word "assets." On the top right side write the word "liabilities." Draw a line under each, and number off five spaces below. Under "assets," fill those five spaces with five pluses that you recognize about yourself. Examples would be "good attitude, hard worker, organized," and so on. Be honest with yourself. Under the heading, "liabilities," write down five negatives about yourself. An example might be "laziness," or "an 'I don't care' attitude," or possibly, "I don't know what I want out of life."

After you evaluate your pluses and minuses, the object is to eliminate the negatives.

On the same page, under your assets and liabilities, answer the following question, "What am I really committed to?" Put three lines under that, although you may find it difficult to fill in three things you're really committed to. This tells you what's important to you and what your priorities are, and even gives you a hint about your goals. The saddest thing is being unable to come up with one solitary commitment, something that you are one-hundred-percent, totally committed to.

At the bottom of the page, leave enough room to answer this question, "How do I see myself ten years from now?" Explain this in a few sentences. Visualize what you want to be ten years from now. The really good thing about this question is that it applies to any age. One time at a seminar I asked that question and there were two gentlemen in the room who were over ninety-six years old. (When you think about it, that probably wasn't a good question to ask a ninety-six-year-old!) When I posed the question, I saw one of them move toward the podium. As he approached me, he asked, "Coach Teaff, would you like to know what I wrote down to answer the question?"

I said, "I would very much like to know what you wrote down."

With a big smile on his face, his crackly old voice made it clear that he was a gentleman of humor and insight. He said, "I wrote down that I just hope I can see myself ten years from now."

Humor aside, the whole idea is really to visualize what you want. That's how you should see yourself. You set a picture, and you work to create that image.

When you've completed this exercise of self-evaluation and analysis, you're on the road to becoming self-motivated.

"To try and get the kids to understand about building on their strengths, I think it's important to tell the kids to look around the classroom," said Don. "Then I tell them, 'You're all different. Not one of you looks the same. Therefore, you may all end up with different jobs, you may find you've got different talents, you'll have different things that motivate you. So I suggest you get to know you. You may not be the best person on a particular machine, but you may be really good at going to the computer and drawing something on the CAD program. You don't have to do the same things that this other person does well, you just have to do the things you can do well, and so let's work on those things.' Maybe a student can't read very well, but he or she can make a particular part just by my telling them how to do it. You've got to accentuate the good things that a student has, and to do that, you have to help them discover what they are."

Step Two to Self-Motivation: Using Mental Pictures

When I left Angelo State to become Baylor's new head coach in 1972, I left a dream office and facility. In my time there, the president of Angelo State had allowed me to help design a new football field house and offices for our staff. The first time I saw Baylor's facilities, I got a big knot in my stomach. The contrast was stunning. Baylor's facilities were nothing like Angelo State's facilities, and not even in the same league as those at Texas Tech, where I'd coached prior to going to Angelo State. All of Baylor's football facilities and athletic department facilities were under the east side of Baylor Stadium. Concrete blocks had been used to build one room after another, with window-unit air conditioning and an eternally musty smell.

However, I was not deterred by the poor facilities, and took the challenge to coach for Baylor. During the first seventeen years of my coaching career at Baylor I was disappointed when several high school players told me they would have loved to come to Baylor, but wouldn't make that choice because their high schools had had better facilities. In all those years I never complained, but continued to sell the philosophy and the university, and did the best I could. But I never ceased to dream. In fact, I pictured a facility at the north end of Baylor Stadium. At the time there was just a parking lot with some end-zone seating there. But over a period of years I constructed in my mind a building that would rise above the north end zone, add a great quality to the stadium, and contain functional rooms and offices, dressing rooms, and a large, large weight room. (The weight room at Baylor in 1972 consisted of one universal gym, an antiquated, outdated piece of equipment that most folks wouldn't have in their home, much less in a facility in which you were supposed to train athletes.) So I dreamed about such a facility.

Finally, when we had the money to build the end-zone facility, I wanted the head football coach's office and the athletic director's office to be identical. My mental picture of those offices had large glass windows on one wall looking out over Baylor Stadium. In fact, after the building was pretty well under construction, I was going through it and walked into what was to be the head football coach's office. Contractors' sketchings on the floor showed that there was to be a closet opening into the head coach's office. That cut down on wall space and eliminated the place in which I had planned to hang certain pictures. I met with the builder and he was able to change the opening of the closet to the hallway, thus maintaining the wall space. Dreams die hard. I wanted those pictures on that particular wall.

Remember, *Psychocybernetics* states that the mind cannot differentiate between that which is vividly imagined and that which is performed. Successful golfers picture their most difficult shots before they hit them. Babe Ruth could not only see the home run going over the fence, but on one occasion he confidently pointed to the area where the ball would go over the fence. The average football player is better when he pictures himself successful and vividly imagines each play before the game starts. Collectively, members of a football team can vicariously experience the invigorating feeling of victory even before the game starts. It's the second best feeling to actually winning the game. That feeling will give a confidence that cannot be attained in any other way.

Our minds can create negative or positive pictures. Control the mental pictures and you control your actions.

> *"I had a mental image of what the computer lab I was setting up would look like with all the kids working at it, and obviously it worked." said Bob. "But with the students*

*themselves, I only help them visualize in a
practical, rather mundane way. I'll tell them to
visualize the math problems before they work
them out, but I've never had them visualize
themselves being successful."*

Step Three to Self-Motivation: Setting Goals

You have to know where you're going before you get
there, so goals become a major factor in self-motivation.
Goals allow you to determine what you want to use as your
incentive motivators. Go back to the story of the little boy
who wanted to be a coach. When he set that as a goal, each
of his involvements after that became tempered by his
vision of the overall major goal. For instance, in planning
an academic curriculum for a degree, he knew a teaching
field was important. He knew that a minor in business and
a master's degree in administrative education would be
helpful, and work in radio and television to improve
communication would be of great assistance.

All this because of a single goal? Yes. And because
of what goal-setting had done for my life, I decided I would
teach goal-setting to every young man who played for me
during my coaching career. I devised a system that was
easy to teach and easy to understand. I would ask each
freshman to fill out a goal card, and then I would sit down
and go over his goals with him. These goals were primarily
for his freshman year. I always asked each freshman,
"What is your major goal for your freshman year?" You'd be
surprised at some of the answers I got. I remember several
young men looking me in the eye and saying, "Why, I want
to win the Heisman Trophy my freshman year." My answer was, "A good goal is to try to make the travel squad
as a freshman."

But one answer was so profound that I continue to

use it as an example of ultimate goal-setting. Before Mike Singletary became the great Chicago middle linebacker, he was a freshman linebacker for Baylor. As a freshman, he came into my office for a goal-setting session. At the end of our session, I asked, "Mike, what is your major goal for your freshman year?" He looked up at me with those intense eyes and said in his soft-spoken manner, "I would like to make a positive contribution to our football team this year."

Wow! What a goal! If every freshman had set the same goal, we probably would have had the best football team in the history of Baylor University.

To make a positive contribution, one must have a positive attitude. I saw that positive attitude in Mike's work habits, his intensity, and his commitment to learning what the college football game was all about. Prior to the eighth game of Mike's freshman year in 1977, we had an open date. We decided to change defenses because of a series of injuries to a particular position. The change brought about a need for a middle linebacker, and Mike Singletary was inserted as the starting middle linebacker prior to the Arkansas game. In that game, his preparation for making a positive contribution paid great dividends. He had twenty-eight unassisted tackles and held Lou Holtz's offense to one of the lowest outputs ever. And from that moment forward, history in the SWC was going to be rewritten. Mike went on to become three times all-SWC Conference, three times all-American, three times captain of the team, and two-time winner of the Davey O'Brien Award, given at that time to the outstanding football player in the southwest part of the United States. A very positive contribution to the team!

To help you set your goals, take a piece of paper, and on the upper right side, write your name. On the left side draw a line. Under the line put "Ultimate goal." Out beside that, put a bracket. In that bracket goes the category in which you'll be setting a goal. The categories will include physical, mental, social, financial, athletic, family, or any other area you feel needs an ultimate goal. On the left side again, put this heading, "Ways that I might reach my ultimate goal."

Now, draw five straight lines and number them one through five. You will use these on which to write down the ways you plan to reach your ultimate goal. After writing them down, prioritize them. Do this by putting another heading, "Priorities," with five spaces underneath. Now take the five ways you've written down and move them around, placing the most important means to reaching your goal on the first line. Then continue with the second, third, fourth, and fifth. By prioritizing your methods, you will place great emphasis on the most important and use those first.

Finally, at the bottom of the page, write down the day, the month and the year you expect to reach your ultimate goal.

The means that you choose to reach your ultimate goal are merely goals within goals. You could refer to those as immediate goals, things that have to be done now for you to succeed later. If your ultimate goal is to receive an "A" in a particular class, your immediate goals might read like this.

1. Take precise notes in class.
2. Do not procrastinate on daily assignments.
3. Approach each class period with a positive attitude.
4. Commit the appropriate time to daily study.
5. Sit on the front row and listen to every word said.

The next step is to analyze the importance of each one of the immediate goals and then prioritize them in a new order, one through five. Now you have a prioritized set of goals to help you reach your ultimate goal.

Aubrey Schulz learned to become a goal-setter, and became a self-motivated individual. Not only did he set a goal to become the starting center at Baylor University, but his other goals were to become all-Southwest Conference and all-American. Lofty goals for a young man who was not a starter at the time, and who really was too small to achieve those goals. However, through personal dedication to achieving those ultimate goals, Aubrey worked extra hard throughout the summer and came back in good enough shape to achieve the starting offensive center position.

Through the same type of determination, he reached his goal of becoming all-SWC Conference. And, since the team won the SWC championship, Aubrey played in the game against SMU on national television. At the time, SMU had a very large all-American nose guard by the name of Louis Kelcher. In that game, as the TV cameras focused in on Louis Kelcher, the viewing audience and the voters for all-American saw a young man from Baylor University playing an outstanding game against one of the great players in the nation. By his efforts in that game, Aubrey propelled himself into the position of first-team all-American center.

Goals can serve as guidelines and direction-finders in our lives. Sometimes when we lose sight of our ultimate goals, they can be used to get us back on the right path. This was the case for Aubrey Schulz. Aubrey's ultimate career goal was to become a head coach on the high-school level. Not only a head coach on a high-school level, but specifically a head coach in one of the largest-division high schools—then the 4A division—in Texas.

One morning the director of the dormitory called me, quite disturbed, and told me that Aubrey had caused a problem in the dorm the night before. He also said that though there was no real proof that Aubrey had been the instigator of other similar incidents, Aubrey might be kicked out of the dorm if he made one more mistake. That probably would have caused me to suspend Aubrey from the football program, and he might even have been suspended from the school.

Aubrey already had gone to his first class when I sent word over to have him come to my office as soon as class was over. Shortly after, Aubrey walked into my office and sat down in front of my desk. He did not know that I had been informed about the incident that had taken place the preceding night. In that incident, someone from an upper floor in the dormitory had dropped a trash basket full of water onto a passerby. Everybody had been laughing and having fun about it, but the dorm director had thought it was dangerous, inappropriate, and grounds for probation.

So I reached into my desk and pulled out Aubrey's goal card. Without saying a word, I passed it across my desk to Aubrey. He took it, and I said, "Read that out loud." Aubrey read aloud the goal card that indicated that his ultimate goal professionally was to be a Division-4A high-school head coach in the state of Texas. A clear, concise goal.

I said, "Aubrey, your behavioral patterns in the dormitory are not conducive to your reaching your ultimate goal. Your conduct has put you in the position for a possible suspension from the dorm and ultimately from our football program. How do you think you will reach your goal of being a head high-school coach if you're no longer at Baylor University, and no longer on this team?"

Aubrey looked at me and said, "Coach, I was just having fun. I didn't mean any harm."

I said, "Aubrey, your actions must reflect your goals, even on a daily basis. A lack of attention to what it takes to get where you want to go will ultimately lead to failure."

Aubrey's head dropped, and then his eyes turned up to me, "I understand exactly what you're saying, and I promise you will never have another problem with me. I want to reach my goals."

I never had another problem with Aubrey, and he went on to reach the goals he had set. Above and beyond the attainment of all-American status and helping lead Baylor to its first SWC conference championship in fifty years, Aubrey Schulz has been a successful head high-school coach in the top division—now 5A—in Texas for many years.

"I use goal-setting in my classroom in the beginning of the year," said Don. "I give the students a piece of paper and ask them to write down what they expect to accomplish in this class, and the progress they're going to make. I help them out by giving them a list of things that they can do. They write a number of things down, and I tell them that, at the end of the year, when they take out their goal list, they'll have a way to measure their progress. Then, if they see they wrote down twelve things at the beginning of the year and have only accomplished six, they have to decide whether their goals were a little too high, or whether they could really have accomplished all twelve if they had worked harder.

"I have the students set the goals and then assess themselves and what they have accomplished as part of a grade, and it works out well. It helps them to be responsible, and to be accountable for what they do or fail to do."

"We set weekly goals with our kids so that they can measure their progress," said

> *Joyce. "And I try to set long-term goals with the kids, but I find that when I try to help the students be a little more realistic in their approach, maybe suggesting that they go to a community college, sometimes they think I'm telling them they're not good enough to go to a university. So I have to be very careful in the way I say this."*

Step Four to Self-Motivation: Taking Care of Business

Each player and coach involved in my last season at Baylor in 1992 received a commemorative ring. There were a lot of symbols on the ring to remind the 1992 team of their successful year and their victory over the University of Arizona in the John Hancock Bowl. There were other symbols that related not only to the 1992 team, but to all the teams going back to 1972.

On the crown of the ring are the words, "John Hancock Bowl Champions." On the outer perimeter of the crown are these words, *From pride to excellence.* This is significant of the fact that the program at Baylor began with the basic of pride. The 1992 team was playing for a so-called lame-duck coach, and was not supposed to be very good. All they took into the season was pride. The 1992 team moved during the season from pride to excellence, just as our football program had done over twenty-one years. It had started with pride and ended with excellence.

On the side of the ring are the initials, "TCB." Every player who ever played for me knows that those initials stand for "Taking Care of Business." It's on the ring to remind the 1992 players that by taking care of business on and off the field, they were able to achieve goals as a team that no one believed they could achieve, even to the point of upsetting the last two teams they played, the University of Texas and one of the top-ranked teams in the nation, the University of Arizona.

"Taking care of business" signifies that at all times, we must be aware of our accountability on and off the field of athletics, in and out of the classroom, in our homes or dorms, or out on the street. Wherever we are, we are responsible for taking care of the appropriate business.

At the end of practice every day, I would talk with the team briefly to remind them of certain obligations related to football or their responsibilities on campus. I usually ended my announcement with the initials, TCB. Taking care of business invokes in an individual the mental approach that we are accountable in all facets of life. Indeed, we are responsible for our actions and thus for the results of those actions. Finger-pointing and blaming someone else for our shortcomings and our failures do not lead to success. If it relates to you, it's your business; take care of it.

*"In cooperative learning situations,"
said Wade, "one of the students in the group
may not be able to do a certain math problem,
but he may have the ability to do the hands-on
stuff. So the students learn to work as a team
and to get on with one another. Some of the
students have to really rethink their approach.
Just this morning, one of the students came to
me and said, 'Mr. Grove, there's this one girl in
the group who doesn't know anything, and I
have to do all the work for her.' I said, 'Well,
good, Brian. What this is going to do is force
her to learn before the unit test. Now it's your*

*responsibility to transfer part of your knowl-
edge to her.' Brian got quiet, and then he said,
'Well, okay.' But I could tell that he was struggling to realize that, as part of the group, each
member was responsible for its overall success."*

21.
Positive Reminders

A famous proverb says, "As we think, so shall we become." This means that what you think about is what becomes your obsession, and what your obsession is dictates who you are and what you want out of life. (Bill Glass, an all-Pro defensive end from the Cleveland Browns, has spent his life since pro ball teaching others. He's been deeply involved in a ministry working with prisons all across America. Bill Glass is a man who has a positive effect on everyone he comes in contact with. He agrees with the overall meaning of the proverb, but I heard him say one time that it wasn't exactly right, because when he was fifteen years old, all he thought about was girls, and he never became one!) The overall point, of course, is still valid. If you think about something, you're more likely to focus on and achieve that. Therefore, what you need to train yourself to do is think about your goals and how you can reach those goals, and have your mind constantly working in a positive way on your behalf.

In the spring of 1979, after a disastrous 1978 season, I was left on a one-year contract, and our backs were literally to the wall to try to get our football program back on a winning track. We'd had an outstanding spring.

Our players had worked extremely hard and had set some lofty goals for the 1979 season. Each player carefully had constructed his own personal goals and the team goals. To reach those goals physically, each player knew he had to work out very hard over the summer.

Since the players lived in different parts of Texas, I knew that the team concept of everyone motivating each other to work out would not work. They had to be individually self-motivated to work out so they would be capable of reaching their individual goals and thus the team goals. After thinking about it, I came up with an idea that I thought could be used by every player and every coach to remind them of their daily and ultimate goals when they could not remind each other.

When spring practice was over I invited all of the freshman players—who were going to be sophomores the next year—to come out to my house to talk about the 1979 season, to have some cookies, and just to spend some time together. We had a great time that night, and devoured a lot of Donell's cookies. Then, as it came time for everybody to leave, I called all the freshmen together and asked them to sit on the floor in my den.

That afternoon I had prepared myself for this moment. I had gone to the equipment room and taken a hole punch and a strip of helmet tape. Baylor's colors are green and gold, and I had chosen the gold helmet tape. I had punched out several hundred little gold dots, put them in a container, and stuck the container in my pocket. I had told no one, not even my coaches, what I was doing.

That night as all the players were gathered around me, I said that, to commemorate our excellent spring practice and to allow all of us the opportunity to be together in a sense and to be encouraged to reach our individual goals throughout the summer, I had formed an organization and they would be the first members inducted into it.

The freshmen's eyes widened as I held up a tiny

gold dot, peeled the back off, and placed it over the six at the bottom of my watch. I turned my wrist to the group so that they could see the gold dot and where I'd placed it. I said, "Tonight, as I place this dot on your watch, you will officially become a member of the Secret Society of the Gold Dot. 'Secret Society' means that you cannot tell anyone what this dot means. Only you and your teammates will know, once they have been told by me. You cannot tell your coaches, you cannot tell the upperclassmen, you cannot tell anyone on campus, you cannot even tell your mama or your daddy. You will be asked many times, 'What is that gold dot on your watch?' You are to simply say, 'I am a member of the Secret Society of the Gold Dot.'"

I meticulously peeled the back off each dot as I placed it over the six on each freshman's watch. Then I said, "Now, as you look at your watch during the day to determine the time, you will see the gold dot. It will remind you of the goals that you've set personally and as a team. It will remind you to do on a daily basis things that will allow you to be successful.

"The color of the dot is gold. Each letter of the word 'gold' stands for something very significant. The 'G' stands for the goals you have set, individually and collectively. You know what those team goals are; you know your own goals. Put them on a card and carry them with you each day, so that every time you look at your watch you will be reminded to take out your goal card and review your goals. Soon they will become second nature to you.

"The 'O' stands for oneness. Many times, I've seen teams overcome great adversity and go on to become successful because the individuals on the team were close and cared for each other and created the oneness their opponents did not have. That oneness must be created in our team for the 1979 season—a oneness that only a cohesive, caring group of team members can create.

"The 'L' stands for loyalty. It is the foundation of all

success. If you are loyal to your goals—both personal and team—if you are loyal to your teammates, recognizing that though they may be many miles away from you, they are accomplishing their goals just as you are accomplishing yours, then you cannot let them down. You must be loyal. You must be loyal to your coaches, to the philosophy of the organization concerning our offense, our defense, and our kicking game. You must be loyal to the students and alumni who back you and depend on you to be the best you can be.

"The 'D' stands for determination. It is an intangible that we all possess and that, when used properly, brings success to our doorstep. Be determined to do on a daily basis the things that will allow you to come back in the fall properly prepared so that this team can reach its goals.

"G-O-L-D. The Secret Society of the Gold Dot."

The next day, as those freshmen walked around campus and joined in their meetings prior to the workout that afternoon, coaches and upperclassmen kept asking, "What's that gold dot?" The freshmen would smile, and say, "I am a member of the Secret Society of the Gold Dot. I'm sorry. I can't say anything more about it." Of course, the more they refused to talk about it, the more interest there was.

That night I had the sophomores—the juniors-to-be for the 1979 season—over to my house. I repeated the same procedure, and the next day we had freshmen and sophomores walking around campus with gold dots on their watches.

The next night I had the juniors—seniors-to-be—over, and by the time they arrived they knew that something had been happening at our house other than the consumption of cookies. They were anxious to know what it was as I began talking about the Secret Society of the Gold Dot. Smiles creased their faces as they extended their arms for me to place the gold dots on their watches.

Finally, at a staff meeting I informed the coaches. They proudly began to wear their gold dots, and soon everyone on campus was asking the question, "What do the gold dots on the football players' watches mean?" An article appeared in the school paper asking the same question. That became a further reminder to the players of their daily responsibility to reach their goals. Those sophomores and juniors went on the next two years to win eighteen games while losing only four. They were champions of the Peach Bowl and played Alabama in the Cotton Bowl after becoming the undefeated SWC champions in 1980.

From 1979 through 1992, a large green banner with a gold dot hung in the center of our dressing room in Baylor Stadium. A similar banner was carried to every road game. Every Baylor freshman football class was initiated into the Secret Society of the Gold Dot. The gold dot banner hangs today in my conference room at the offices of the American Football Coaches Association. It reminds me and all of my staff members of our daily goals and our ultimate goals. Corporations, businesses, and even political groups have used the concept of the gold dot to further their mental commitment to success.

> *"I use some props in the lab as reminders," said Don. "They're cartoon safety posters of a guy who's always getting hurt. There's one of a compressed air cylinder going through a wall with a guy riding on it. It's pretty funny, but it does remind the kids that we're using potentially dangerous equipment, and they need to remember the safety rules."*

I've used other such concepts to make my point about what it takes to be the member of a strong team. In 1992, for example, I went down to the hardware store and purchased about thirty feet of chain, the links of which were about an inch and a quarter long and about an inch wide. Made of solid steel, the chain was designed to hoist heavy, heavy loads. But it was appropriate for my needs as well. After purchasing the chain, I asked if there were a bolt cutter available in the hardware store. The proprietor gave me a strange look, but said, "Yes, over there."

I asked, "May I use it to cut up this chain?"

You should have seen the look on his face then.

I took two brown paper bags over to the bolt cutter and started to cut the chain. I found that it takes three links to make one complete link; you have to cut two of them to get one. Soon the sacks were filled, one with cut-up links, and the other with solid, sound links. Then I left the store and returned to Baylor.

That afternoon, in a meeting, I began to talk about the importance of our team and our team goals, and how each person, by reaching his own individual goals, could contribute to the strength of the team, much like a chain, each of whose links reflects the strength of the overall chain.

The next day, I had a plaque made up with a piece of the chain mounted on it. The sign under the chain said, "No chain is stronger than its weakest link." I put that up over the door leading out of the meeting room, and again discussed with the team the importance of each individual link. At the team meetings the next day, I asked the team captains for both the offense and defense to come to the front of the room. I pulled out a shiny link, explained to each one of the team members that this was what made up the team, and that for our team to succeed and reach the goals we had set for ourselves, each member had to commit to becoming the best he could be in all areas.

The procedure for receiving a link was simple, I told them. Only the head coach would determine who received one, and he would present it in front of the squad, or at a private moment. The individual receiving the link could carry it in his pocket, put it on his desk, or wear it around his neck. It was his link, and evidence of how important he was to the overall team.

I then gave a link to J. J. Joe, our offensive team captain, who had demonstrated all the qualities necessary to be a team leader and to be a strong link in the chain of success. Then I gave one to Mike McFarland, our defensive team captain. Mike had come from East Texas, a young man who gave everything he had every day in every way. He was the epitome of what a strong link should be in Baylor's chain of success.

It was a good ten days before I gave my next link to anyone. That day, I walked up after practice to a player who had had an especially good workout, and reached out to shake his hand. When he grabbed my hand, a smile spread over his face as he felt the link in my palm. He took it and gripped it tightly in his right hand.

The next day, I gave three more. The following day, four. But by our first ball game, a majority of the players still did not have a link. On the Friday before our first game, I called them all together and presented a walk-on with a shiny link. I used this opportunity to explain that a player didn't have to be a starter or even play in the game to be a critical link in the chain of success. The walk-on receiving the link had proven to me through his effort and attitude that he was making a strong contribution to the potential success of our team.

The following Monday afternoon, two of the assistant coaches came up to me and said that some of their players were concerned that they had not received their link. The players had asked the assistants what they had to do to be recognized as a strong link. I told the coaches to emphasize to the players, "No chain is stronger than its weakest link. Therefore, if we are to have the strongest team possible, each player must be at his best."

The very next day, I gave out five links after evaluating film and watching the practice of those same individuals. The third week, I gave another fifteen, because by now we were really rolling as a team and every player and coach was trying to be the best he could possibly be.

Three points emerged from the "strongest link" concept: (1) The importance of each individual and his contribution toward the success of the team was emphasized. (2) When recognized, the individual received great satisfaction from having been pointed out as a strong link. (3) The link was something for others to see, but it was also something tangible for the individual receiving the link to hold on to.

22.
Psychological Ploys

Although self-motivation is by far the best form of motivation, psychology plays a great role in human endeavor, and what sometimes is thought to be motivation can turn out to be merely a psychological ploy. Psychological ploys are instantaneous methods of motivating individuals, groups, or teams with a one-time jolt. The problem is that this type of motivation does not last, and individuals sometimes will come to rely on someone else psychologically motivating them to do something. But, although there is a downside to this type of motivation, I have found it to be quite effective on a number of occasions.

In 1976, for example, we had taken our football team from Baylor to play the University of Michigan in Ann Arbor. Michigan had not lost a home game in several years and certainly were expecting to defeat the Baylor Bears. In addition, there were 106,000 fans present, of whom probably only two thousand were Baylor fans.

Our team members, knowing the reputation of Michigan, had been somewhat tentative all week long and obviously were concerned about the great number of fans and the noise they would hear in the stadium. Earlier in the week, while looking at Michigan's previous game with

Stanford, I had watched as they let the camera run prior to the team going onto the field. I noticed that the opposing team—the University of Stanford—came onto the field from the west side. That's the side where both the home and the visiting dressing rooms are located. In fact, the dressing rooms—both the Michigan and the visiting—are across from each other. I also noticed that, immediately after the opposing team had come out on the sideline and started stretching a little prior to kickoff, the stadium had suddenly erupted as the Michigan team came onto the field and ran right by the Stanford team.

The psychology here was that, as the Michigan Wolverines came charging out of the tunnel and ran right by their opponents, the stadium erupted with 106,000 people screaming for their home team and intimidating the opposing team.

Having discovered this little secret of Michigan's, I decided to throw them a curve ball. On Tuesday afternoon after practice, I shared with the players what I had discovered and told them that we would turn the tables on the University of Michigan. We would stay in our dressing room until the University of Michigan went out onto the field, then we would follow right behind them. As the crowd erupted, screaming for Michigan, we would come right in behind them. It would thus seem as if we were at home and the people were screaming for us, and our players would not be intimidated. They would know we were pulling something on Michigan.

The players smiled, clapped, and felt good about the plan, which we reiterated each day of the week. Finally, on Thursday, before the Friday when we would fly out to Michigan, I told the players that the only way our plan would work was if we were psychologically prepared to wait in that dressing room for as long as thirty minutes before the game started. We'd have to be relaxed, we couldn't be hyper, and we couldn't be anticipating running out on the field and getting the game started. We had to be completely in control of our emotions. They all said that they could do that.

So on Saturday after the normal warm-up, the Baylor Bears went back into their dressing room. After some last-minute instructions, I told the players to find a comfortable position on the floor or up against the wall, the head trainer turned off the lights, and one of the managers turned on some very pleasant, relaxing music.

Ten minutes before kickoff, the door cracked open. An official stuck his head into the quiet, darkened dressing room and called my name. I answered by saying, "I'm over here."

He walked toward me, stepping over the players lying around on the floor and said, "Coach, it's time to get on the field."

I said, "We've decided that we would like to have Michigan go out first and then we will follow."

He said, "You can't do that. It's tradition. You have to go out first."

I said, "I know. I discovered the tradition, and we're going out second."

He turned around and walked out of the room, evidently going over to where Coach Bo Schembechler and his team were waiting for us to go out on the field. The official told them we would not budge. Evidently, Coach Schembechler sent him back to tell me that we needed to get our team out on the field.

I said, "Look. We're relaxed. Everything is really fine here, and we're prepared to wait all afternoon if we need to. *We* are going on the field second."

The official turned, and after a few seconds we could hear some yelling and the slamming of a few helmets up against the metal door as the Michigan players reluctantly started out the tunnel to the field.

I said, "Okay, men, let's go."

As soon as the last Michigan player filed past our door, our captains led the Baylor team right out behind them. Michigan ran out onto the field to the yells of 106,000 people, and our Baylor team followed right in behind them. We turned right onto our own bench, and prepared to play the game psychologically ready to go. We played an outstanding game, and although the score ended in a 10-10 tie, we actually dominated both the offense and the defense.

Did that psychological ploy have an effect on our team? I think it did. It gave our team something up on an opponent who had all the advantages of playing at home.

Another situation occurred where a psychological ploy had a great effect on the outcome of a game. At the time, I was the head football coach at McMurry College, a small Methodist school in Abilene, Texas. One of our big opponents was cross-town rival, Abilene Christian University. It was the last game of the season, and we had had a relatively poor season. Of course, ACU was having a great year, and two or three of their players actually would be drafted to the NFL. McMurry had lost against ACU for three straight years, and we were a heavy underdog to lose this fourth consecutive time.

We were the McMurry College Indians, and at homecoming, our sororities and fraternities had built a tepee village. With great authenticity, they had built the campfires and tepees and all the regalia. And in keeping with the Indian theme, the student body always chanted before each game something that sounded like, "Allah, cumba." ("Cumba" was supposed to be an Indian word meaning "victory.")

At the beginning of the week, I started talking to our players about the tradition of "cumba." I told them that we would have a victory on the fourth try. It would be Cumba Four. I also mentioned this at an early press conference during the week, so that the headlines of the local paper read, "McMurry coaches and players believe in Indian tradition of 'Cumba'—victory."

Victory on the fourth try. Things were set up the way I wanted them to be. But I hadn't yet finished. There's a place in Abilene called *Athletic Supply*. The guys there were great friends and supplied our football team with all the athletic equipment we needed. On Friday afternoon, I got to the store just at closing time. I pulled two of my friends aside, and said, "Look, I have a request to make that's going to take some after-hours work. It's also got to be done in complete secrecy. Will you do it for me?" I explained that I wanted to create a new jersey to be worn as a surprise in the football game against ACU.

I explained how I wanted each jersey to look, and what I wanted on it. They committed to doing the job, and the two of them stayed up all Friday night and into Saturday morning completing the jerseys. Then they boxed them and secretly put them in the back of my car. I had told one student manager of the secret, and had instructed him to go into the dressing room while we were on the field for our warm-up prior to the game, and to hang one of the new jerseys in the locker of each of the players.

Again, ACU was a big and talented team. We were young and not very good at that time, so when we came back into the dressing room, the players were expecting me to try and say something to motivate them for this one occasion. Instead, when they walked in, their eyes became as large as silver dollars. There hung the new jerseys, and they were turned so that each player could see his name on the back of the jersey. (To my knowledge, that was the first time names ever appeared on the backs of jerseys.) They picked them up and turned them around, and there on the front, across the top above the numbers, was "Cumba Four."

I explained that the new jerseys would let everyone in the stands know who they were, not just by number but by name, and the fans would be watching every play that

199

each individual player made. I said, "When our team goes on the field and ACU lines up in front of us, whether it's on offense or defense, what they are going to see is a reminder that we are going to win this game. Victory on the fourth try. Cumba Four."

The guys were so excited that they played well above their talent level and won the game, 9-8, a one-point victory that was as good as a fifty-point victory. The McMurry College Indians had lived up to Cumba Four. Victory on the fourth try.

One other time ranks right up there with Cumba Four. It is, perhaps, the most famous psychological ploy used in the annals of college football. It occurred in 1978, before the last game of a miserable season. The 1978 season had loomed large on the horizon for the Baylor football program. We had recruited well, and had great players ready to play this season for a SWC championship. But we had one major problem. Our road schedule for non-conference games was extremely tough. We had to play the University of Georgia, the University of Kentucky, and Ohio State on three consecutive weekends. We lost all three by less than 10 points total, but received several key injuries to some of our top players. This put us in a tailspin from which we never really recovered.

Even though we won an enormous victory on the road against Texas A&M that year, we could not psychologically turn the season around and win consistently. Injuries and negative thought lines kept us from becoming successful. We played Rice University in the next to last game of the season, and were unceremoniously beaten. That made us 2 and 8 for the season. Coming back on the bus from Houston, I knew that our season had been a disaster and that if we didn't do something to turn it around for the last ball game, our whole program could end up a disaster.

Our last game was to be against the University of

Texas, then the ninth-ranked team in the nation and already selected to play in the Sun Bowl in El Paso, Texas. Early reports were that Texas would destroy the devastated Baylor team by as many as forty points. Coming back on the bus with a strong resolve to turn our season around and give us momentum for recruiting, I formed a plan.

First, at a meeting with the players on Sunday afternoon, I told them we were going to win the game against Texas. But in order for us to accomplish that very large goal, each individual had to think and act like a winner. That would not be easy, because we had been losing, but we could change our attitude. Second, we devised a game plan for the Texas game, one that included a running back at quarterback, and an offensive plan that included the option. We made some changes defensively that the players liked, and they had a good week of work. They began to expect to win.

However, on Thursday I became concerned that something else was needed. So, after practice, I related a story about two Eskimos who fished on solid ice in the northern area of Alaska. While using the same equipment, fishing two feet apart with the same size hole cut in the ice, one fisherman was successful, while the other failed.

The failing fisherman asked the successful one, "What is the secret of your success?"

The successful fisherman turned and looked at him, and mumbled, "You've got to keep the worms warm."

I stuck my tongue in my lower lip as I made that statement to give the impression that the fisherman's mouth was full of worms. The reaction of the players was, to say the least, lukewarm. But the point I was emphasizing was that they had to be willing to do whatever it took to get the job done. Though it might be distasteful or painful, if they wanted to win, someone had to rise to the occasion and "keep the worms warm."

By Friday, the team was still wavering. I felt they

would perform well at the beginning of the game, but the first fumble we made or the first touchdown that Texas scored would be a death knell for the success of the game. Accordingly, I hit upon a plan.

On Saturday morning at the team devotional, I reminded the team they had a game plan that would work, they had started to think like winners, and I fully believed they knew what was necessary to get the job done. To keep the momentum going, I retold the story of the Alaskan fishermen, and what it had taken to catch fish in the frigid lake. Then I dismissed them to go to their various offensive and defensive meetings and to tape, and I left the stadium.

I stopped at two small grocery stores and asked if they kept any great big fishing worms, and received puzzled negatives from the people there, who recognized me and probably thought I had lost my mind. Here I was, just hours before a big game, asking about fishing bait! I tried two other stores with no success before I drove to Lake Waco and finally found a store that had big night crawlers, about six inches long and as thick as my finger. I bought some of them, drove back to the stadium, took one of them into the office, went into the bathroom and washed it with shampoo, then popped it into a little plastic container.

In the dressing room prior to the game, I held my little friend firmly in my left hand. Just as we were about to go out on the field, I stepped up on a bench. The players gathered around. "I've never been associated with a team that had a better week of preparation," I said. "However, it will take more than preparation to win today. Someone on that field has to do whatever it takes to win the game. The game now belongs to you players; there's very little that we as coaches can do."

After a dramatic pause, I continued, "But there's one thing that I'm willing to do, and that is to keep the worms warm."

I reached into my left hand, jiggled the worm a couple of times, and popped him into the corner of my mouth, letting him hang over my lip. The team started yelling, and I pointed toward the field. They turned and rushed out the door, and I removed my little friend from the corner of my mouth and dropped him in the trash.

One of the assistant coaches, Joe Broeker, was standing just outside the door when we left to go to the field. He said as I walked by, "I've never seen a group as excited and relaxed as those guys." I just smiled.

At the opening kickoff, all the coaches and players were smiling and laughing, excited about the game and mentally relaxed.

We won the game, and it changed the course of history for Baylor football. From that moment forward, through the '80s and early '90s, we had the second-best record in football in the Southwest Conference, won another championship, and went to seven Bowls.

The "worm incident" has been misinterpreted hundreds of times. Everyone wants to make it a great motivational act. But it was only a psychological ploy to relax our players and allow them to utilize the plan that had been devised and give them a chance to win against the University of Texas. It may have helped us win the game against Texas, but I believe that if we hadn't laid a good groundwork of mental and physical preparation, the whole incident would have been in vain.

V.
Leadership

*Leadership is physically and mentally
tiring. And most often, worthwhile goals
are the hardest to attain and take
the longest. Therefore, mental and
physical endurance is essential
to a successful leader.*

—Grant Teaff

INTRODUCTION
Leadership Analyzed

In the fall of 1994, as executive director of the American Football Coaches Association, I conducted my first meeting of Division IA head coaches. (The NCAA Division 1A designates the large major universities playing collegiate football.) The next day we took the information gathered from the coaches to the conference commissioners who were among those attending the meeting, as were a large representation of Division 1A athletic directors from across the nation.

One head coach who attended both meetings wrote me a letter that was complimentary of both meetings. In conclusion, the coach made this statement, "I like your style of leadership." I put the letter down and began to think about my "style of leadership." I analyzed my own leadership style for some time and then asked others who have been exposed to my leadership to analyze it. Then I looked at leaders in different walks of life I have read about, come in contact with, or simply observed, and put together a list of the things anyone who wants to prepare to become a leader needs to have.

Preparing to be a leader does not necessarily mean that you will become the head of a large corporation, the head coach at a major college, or the president of the United States. What it means is that you will prepare yourself for any eventuality and will better understand the important role leadership plays in the success of any project or group.

23.
Traits of a Leader

Using the technique of self-evaluation recommended earlier in this book, list your assets and liabilities. If you check your list and have the following assets, you can be well assured that you are eminently qualified to become an outstanding leader in any area:

1. Sincerity. If you're a good actor and can fake sincerity, I suggest that you go into the field of acting and do not consider yourself a candidate for leadership. Sincerity can be faked for only a short span of time, and leadership demands consistency over the long haul. Either you are a sincere person, or you are not.

2. Caring. To me, having a caring attitude or trait can best be described as having a servant's heart. Those who sincerely want to serve others, care. They care about the individuals, they care about their circumstances, and they burn on the inside to do something about them. That doesn't mean that every project has to be a world-changing idea. It simply means that the person best qualified to lead, truly cares.

3. Emotion. Having the trait of emotion means you display sincerity and caring. Although emotions must be controlled, those you are trying to lead must know that you have a fire and intensity within you; that you burn with an emotional zeal to accomplish.

4. Loyalty. I could write an entire book on the importance of loyalty as a leadership trait. I know of no organization or group that's ever been successful over a period of time that did not exhibit the tremendous power we call loyalty. Loyalty must run both ways. There must be loyalty within an organization toward the leader, and loyalty from the leader to those inside the group or organization. Loyalty does not mean that there are no disagreements or opposite opinions. Far from it. Loyalty, simply stated, means that once a decision is made, it is the majority decision or the final decision made by the designated leader, and everyone must work to accomplish the objective of that decision. A person can be disloyal by simply saying nothing, so it's important to remember that there is a time to take a stand for your goals, for your leaders, or for those who are following you.

5. Diplomacy. The adage says, "Discretion is the better part of valor." I think that applies to the concept of diplomacy as a trait. A diplomat should be wise and have a broad view, and should be able to join two separate opinions into one powerful force by finding agreement on certain issues. Being a peacemaker is the role of a diplomat.

6. Dependability. "Solid," "steadfast," "accountable" are all descriptions of a person who is dependable. If a leader lacks this trait—even though he or she may be strong in other areas—the lack of dependability ultimately will keep him or her from achieving the goals set for the group. Being dependable includes being on time and being consistent, in terms of both your personality and your rhetoric.

7. Judgment. Growing up in a small West Texas town, I learned that the term for good judgment was "horse sense." I'm not exactly sure what that means, except that when you're riding a horse out through the far reaches of

West Texas and happen to get lost, you give the horse the reins and he finds his way back to the feed lot. His basic instincts work. Translated, having the good judgment means you use your basic instincts for justice and fairness in the decision-making process, and that works well over time.

8. Enthusiasm. Even while controlling your emotions, there is an appropriate time for a leader to be enthusiastic. A positive attitude brings about strong enthusiasm in you, and excitement about what you're doing or trying to accomplish generates enthusiasm within the group. Enthusiasm alone, however, is not enough, because you can be enthusiastic without being a leader. But being an enthusiastic leader enhances your chances of success.

9. Fairness. Over the years I have developed a basic rule for any project, business deal, or major goal: It must be a win-win-win situation. If you look at every situation under the microscope of fairness, and you make plans and the outcome of those plans is based on fairness, then you create a win-win-win situation.

10. Endurance. A runner with endurance always finishes the race. A leader without endurance literally can be worn down and then will retreat from his intended goals. Leadership is physically and mentally tiring. And, most of the time, worthwhile goals are the hardest to attain and take the longest. Therefore endurance, both mental and physical, is essential to a successful leader.

Leadership traits can be natural or developed. Sometimes, ill-prepared and not fully developed as a person with strong traits, one is thrust into a leadership role. This in no way diminishes the importance of the goals of the project he or she is to complete. Therefore, the person should plan to improve on the job.

The first step to improvement is to recognize leadership traits. Those that you have, use. Those that you lack, develop.

"I've never actually thought of developing leadership skills in my students, but it sounds like a really great idea," said Bob. "I talk to my students about behavior and expectations, and in the classes where students are used to being successful, they very much want to have behavior that I certify as appropriate. So I think they'd respond to learning about leadership."

"I use this every day," said Don. "In the lab we appoint a foreman, and that person has to earn the position. He's like the captain of a football team, or the president of the class. When we clean up at the end of lab, his job is to be sure that it's all done right and if some kid doesn't do his share, he'll tell him to do it or he'll report the student to the boss—me. When we work in small groups in cooperative learning, I tell the students that some will come to the forefront and be the team leaders. I actively encourage this. Then the team leaders have the responsibility of organizing things in the group. They have to give all the grades, too. They sit down with each member of their group and go over a list of questions. The team leader is a leader—not a parent—and the students like it."

"I just let the cream rise to the top, so to speak," said Wade. "I feel that it would be a good idea to start a leadership development course. I've never seen anything like this in education before, and I think its time has come."

24.
Leadership Action

An action is something that you do, as in pushing your own hot button for self-motivation. The action that you take as a leader will push the hot buttons of those you're leading. The following are actions taken by leaders in all walks of life.

Asking others their opinion. Asking for an opinion denotes respect for the individual asked. It says to others, "Your opinion is important and will be considered." It also can give you insights that you might not otherwise reach.

Setting an example. Never ask someone to do something that you yourself are unwilling to do. But the flip side of that is that it's okay to ask someone to do something that you've already done. As an athlete running wind sprints, it always comforted me to know that my coach had run those same wind sprints at another time and in another place. The example of a leader sets the tone for everyone.

Seeking responsibility. There is a thread that runs through all leaders—the thread of seeking responsibility. Responsibility isn't always thrust upon us. Most of the time, we have to seek it. We do this by preparing ourselves and by letting others know that we're willing to take on responsibility.

Taking responsibility for failed efforts. Leaders who point fingers and place blame publicly will not remain in a position of leadership for very long. As a leader, you do everything in your power to try to achieve success. But success is not always possible. In team sports, unless there's a tie, only half the teams are going to win while half are going to lose. A loss can occur because of an uncontrollable factor. This does not mean that you are less of a leader or that your plans were poor from the start, it simply means that on this particular occasion, you failed to reach your goals. Taking responsibility for that failure without playing the martyr will enhance your chances for success at the next attempt.

Giving others the credit. When achieving success, point out the efforts and contributions of others. Everyone knows that you were the leader and that you had a part in the success, but there are many within a group who will be recognized only by your having acknowledged them. The basic philosophy I adhered to was very simple: It doesn't matter who gets the credit as long as the job gets done.

Making sound decisions. Substitute the word "solid" for sound and making such a decision will produce exactly the same action. Solid and sound denote factual and basic, and that type of decision can be made only with the proper information concerning the issues and the problems related to them.

Setting objectives; listening to others' ideas. Many times a leader's responsibility is that of broadly outlining objectives. After setting these broad objectives and directing discussion about them, if you listen to and integrate the ideas of others into the broad objectives, you add a "we" flavor to what you're trying to accomplish.

Having a written plan. Like the rudder on a ship, written plans keep you on course. You also can use them as a yardstick against which to measure your progress and get feedback on your performance. Written plans keep you from putting off action or from becoming stagnant. They keep you focused on your goals and not on the doubts that always occur.

Visualizing the end results. The power to see the full picture and to place in proper perspective your stated goals is extremely important, but one action that I've found to be most helpful is visualizing the end results. This not only fills you with a positive affirmation, but it gives you a mental picture of what you want to attain. Then you can paint the mental picture you have visualized for those working with you to achieve the common goal.

Solving problems. The best way to become a problem-solver is to accept the fact that there are going to be problems with any objective, purpose, or goal. Anticipating those problems allows you to design a plan so that when a problem occurs, you already have a procedure to follow to overcome it. Approach each problem individually and apply the win-win-win theory to each problem. (It's also good to remember not to jump to conclusions. This is an important nonaction to take in relation to problems.)

25.
Requirements for Leadership

There are five requirements for a leader.

First, knowledge. Knowledge built on factual information or evidence is imperative to your presentation of objectives and goals. Knowing the intricacies of modern-day issues and the problems that relate to those issues is critical to your development of a plan. For example, a few years ago I asked the administration and trustees of Baylor University to build new athletic facilities. Their response was positive, since they knew that I always had been willing to work with what I had and had been successful with the poorest facilities in the Southwest Conference. Therefore, when I raised the issue of the new facilities, they knew that I had knowledge of the SWC and expertise in the issues that confronted college football, and that I would not recommend such a bold move if I did not feel that it was the proper thing to do for the future of Baylor football and Baylor athletics. (The completed facilities have added greatly to the stature of the university, its ability to recruit, and the overall success of its athletic program.)

Second, courage. Courage comes from confidence and not blind foolhardiness. Courage allows you to go where others may not have trodden. It allows you to be bold in your pursuit of a cause. It allows you to have no fear.

When I asked Bill Lane, one of my former coaches who had been with me for over twenty-five years, to characterize my style of leadership, he immediately said, "Fearless." I asked him to explain. Bill said, "When you chose to take the Baylor job, many had turned it down for fear they could not be successful. For some reason, you had no doubt. You were not afraid. You were not afraid of failure, and you inspired those of us who came with you to approach the job with the same air of confidence, lacking the fear that keeps one paralyzed.

"Another example of your having no fear centered around Baylor's relationship to the University of Texas," Bill continued. "You exuded respect for their program, but were not intimidated and did not fear the awesomeness of the Burnt Orange—a team from the largest state school in the state of Texas, and from one of the most successful football programs in America. Finally, the key for all of us as coaches was that you prepared our team not to be intimidated or afraid of the perception of Texas, but to prepare for its reality, and to do it with confidence and without fear of failure.

"In conclusion," Bill said, "the proof's in the pudding." Roughly translated, that means that from 1974 through 1992, Baylor won ten of its games with the University of Texas while losing nine.

Third, decisiveness. A leader must be able to make decisions and make them with confidence after having studied the options. Being indecisive or wishy-washy is a ticket straight to failure. A look through the history books will show that key battles were won because the leaders involved were decisive, and fortunes were made for no other reason than that someone made a clear, concise decision. On the other hand, some of the greatest failures in the annals of history have occurred because a leader was indecisive, or waited too long to make a decision. That's applicable to everyday life, also. Looking around, you can see failure after failure. If you were to dig into these, to really analyze them, you'd find that somewhere in each case, a leader had failed to be decisive.

Fourth, communication. Of all the "musts" for a leader this has to rank close to the top. First, listening to others and their opinions is a key part of communication. Listening is an acquired ability, as is a good memory, which can be attained by practice. The addition of a strong memory to the habit of listening empowers you in a way that few experience. It turns you into a communicator, and as a leader, you must be able to communicate your ideas and projects.

The part that listening plays in communication is unique. To illustrate it, let me tell you about a conversation I once overheard between two individuals. This conversation was extremely one-sided. One party was doing all the talking, the other party was doing all the listening. But he was doing it in such a way that he conveyed interest in what was being said. He also acknowledged certain points with brief remarks, so that when the conversation was over, the person who had been doing the talking came up to me and said, "I just had one of the greatest conversations I've ever had. Joe is a real communicator." Actually, Joe was a real listener, and by his intent listening, had made the other party feel that his ideas were received and that they had, in fact, had a great conversation.

To improve your listening skills, you might want to use a trick I learned. Do not formulate in your mind what you're going to say when the person you're having a conversation with finishes what he or she is saying. Wait till they're through, and then respond to what you've heard. You'll find the conversation flows much more freely because you're listening more intently. Another important aspect of communication is to avoid being defensive. If the hair on the back of your head stands up when you are being questioned by someone else, you'll usually find your voice lifting a few pitches. When this happens, you should recognize that you're being antagonized and that you're really not communicating. (You can see this process of antagonization almost any night on television, whether in a sporting interview or a political interview. The interviewer can "get the goat," so to speak, of the guest, forcing him or her to be defensive by the questions asked.) When you find yourself becoming irate at some suggestion or question, you should calmly, coolly, stay with your point and continue to communicate.

Fifth, character (or integrity, trust, or honesty). When the evidence of good character is not sustained by the action of the leader, doubt occurs among those being led. A person's character is not formed in one incident, but rather in an accumulation of incidents. Integrity and character are judged by our actions, our words, and our deeds. One of the great examples of character in a leader was Abraham Lincoln, who was referred to by many as "Honest Abe." Lincoln formed a business partnership in the 1830s that just didn't work out. When the partnership broke up because of the death of the other partner, Lincoln was left with a large debt. He paid back every penny of that debt. Lincoln's stand on the issue of slavery in the divided states put him in a position to be revered by Americans forever. At the time, it was a tough, hard road, but the decision he made was based on his character. He did not believe slavery was correct, and he made a strong stand and had the power to do something about it. Because of his actions, Abraham Lincoln became revered as a leader of strong character.

As a leader, you too will be empowered by your natural and developed traits, the action you take as a leader, and your response to the requirements of leadership. But the sustaining power of leadership can best be summed up in these words, in this poetic fashion:

> Success is in the way you walk the paths
>   of life each and every day,
> It's in the little things you do and in the
>   things you say,
> It's not in reaching heights or fame,
> It's not in reaching goals that all men
>   seek to claim.
> Success is being big of heart, clean, and
>   broad of mind.
> Success is being faithful to your friends,
>   and to the stranger, kind.
> Success is in your teammates, your family, and what they learn from you,
> Success is having character in everything
>   you do.

EPILOGUE

By Tracy Teaff

Coordinator of Special Education
Waxahachie Independent School District

I decided to be a special-education teacher when I was eight years old. Perhaps that will give you some insight into how my father's techniques took root in me at a young age. I learned very early on to set goals for my life, and from the day I decided to be a special-education teacher, my course was unwavering. I tailored my studies, my part-time jobs, and my activities around things I thought would be helpful to my becoming a special-education teacher.

My desire to choose this career was influenced and strengthened by my father's decision to coach at Baylor University. Baylor's football team was regarded as unsuccessful at the time, and it took a lot of hard work to shuck the characterization of "underdog." I know Dad took on the challenge for a lot of reasons, one of which was that he wanted to prove that a "have-not" college *could* be successful if someone cared enough to help the players reach their potential. That had a great deal to do with why I so strongly wanted to help students who have to struggle against many difficulties, and who are usually operating from an "underdog" status.

Growing up as one of the daughters of Grant Teaff forced me to develop a strong sense of identity. I did not want to go through life being known only as "Grant Teaff's daughter." I wanted people to know me as Tracy, even though I was proud to be Dad's daughter. In the first two years of Dad's Baylor job, when the team was not yet winning big, it was sometimes hard to go to school on Mondays, since a lot of criticism and ridicule about the team were bandied about. This evoked mixed feelings in me. I'm glad now that I had to go through it all, because I understand how outside factors affect a child's feelings, concentration, and behavior. As a coach's daughter, I had to learn to take the bad with the good. As part of my response to the situation at school, I learned to develop my leadership skills, and these have been great assets to me in my life and career. Of course, football knowledge was always an asset with the boys at school, because I could talk knowledgeably about the sport, and collected football cards and read the sports pages avidly. That knowledge later helped me to build rapport with my students and to create lesson plans.

When Dad took the job at Baylor, I was thrilled. I wanted him to take the challenge of changing the record at Baylor. Layne, my younger sister, was devastated. Her question was, "How can you want to coach a bunch of *losers?*" Of course, Dad's response was that that was exactly why he wanted to coach them. He wanted to teach them to be winners. That idea appealed to Layne, and she was able to accept the move from San Angelo to Waco.

Dad's career gave us so many opportunities and advantages that it seems ridiculous even to mention the small difficulties it caused, but there were some. Before the team became successful, for example, I had to learn patience with Dad's long-term strategy for Baylor. When it became successful, I had to learn to accept the interruptions we would always have to our meals out, when people would want to talk to Dad or get his autograph. But soon my pride in his accomplishments and respect for his goals and integrity outweighed any impatience I might have had.

Even though Dad's job was time-consuming, I always felt that he was there for us. I think some of that had to do with the fact that I grew up in a home where there was no criticism, or not the kind that I could recognize as criticism, anyway. If criticism occurred, it was constructive, and never left me feeling bad. I think that one of the greatest gifts you can give anyone is a strong sense of self-esteem and individual worth, and that's what my parents did for us. We knew we were loved. We knew we were important. We knew there was always time for us.

We have always been a close-knit family. In fact, we used to refer to ourselves as a team. We were taught to respect each other before we even knew we were being taught. Because I grew up with respect and was able to realize what a great advantage this was, I consider respect to be essential in the classroom. Many times, students have to learn from teachers what it is to be respected and to respect others.

In our family, that respect took many forms. For example, my parents always let me make my own choices. However, that was really not such a big risk because I had already been taught a value system. That value system, then, was the basis for my being able to make good decisions.

Another aspect of the way my parents respected us was that they never belittled or talked down to us. I've accompanied my dad to football practice many times, and never once have I seen him humiliate or denigrate a player or coach. (This is critical to my philosophy of teaching. It's hard to teach respect while talking down to or belittling the students.) Each week I would ask him what plays he was using, what strategy he was going to employ. No matter how busy Dad was, he always answered me, often demonstrating a play I didn't understand, and was always ready to break it down into easier components so I could grasp the overall principle. He coached me.

People have asked me if there was a time when I wished I had a brother, and I've had to laugh and say that I had ninety-six brothers every season. Dad got to know his players very well, and so did all of us in the family. My father was interested in the players' daily lives as well as their academic progress and their development as football players. So looking at the total person was ingrained in me. Mom and Dad were very serious about their responsibilities to each individual student/athlete. That sense of involvement with students has carried over to me as a special-education teacher. I believe that it's vital that you as a teacher know what your students are grappling with at home so you have a basic understanding of the difficulties they face.

For example, one time I was trying to help a teacher take her work with one of my students a little more slowly, and give him concrete instructions and directions, but she was disgusted with the child. "He just doesn't care," she told me. "He comes into my classroom every day, puts his head down on the desk, and sleeps. I'm tired of dealing with him."

I talked and talked with her, trying to explain what this student had to deal with at home, but nothing worked. Finally, I told her I would pick her up after school and take her to the student's house. That afternoon when we arrived at the house, I showed her the bed in which our student slept with three of his brothers. (His sisters slept on the floor.) I was able to get her to realize that, not only did he not get a good night's sleep, but that he and his siblings had to get up and dressed at 4.30 a.m., when his mother went to work. No wonder he fell asleep in class! After this, the teacher was able to look at the child in a new light.

One of the funny things I remember about growing up was the way Dad helped me develop confidence. His strategy was to make up nonsense puzzles while we were in the car and challenge me to work out the answers. He might, for example, tell me that there was a two-ton elephant in Los Angeles and a two-ounce cricket in New York, riding in cars weighing four thousand pounds each. The question was, how long would it take a one-legged grasshopper to kick the warts off a pickle? I would be in the back of that car with my pad and pencil, multiplying and figuring, and I would eventually come up with an answer. Whatever answer I called out, Dad would get really excited and say, "Tracy, how did you do that? You're amazing!"

Some people may not think this is a good way to teach, but the confidence I gained from seeing Dad turn around in awe at my cleverness has never left me. I began to believe I could do anything I set my mind to, including math. Dad's puzzles even taught me critical thinking, because I would sometimes have to say, "Dad, you haven't given me enough information." And he'd say, "You're right. I haven't." And then he would give me another piece of nonsensical information, all the while acting amazed at my astute assessment of the situation.

When the going has gotten tough in my life or my career, as it has from time to time, and I've wavered, wondering if I could make it through one more day, Dad's response has always been, "You can do it!" And, sure enough, it has always turned out that I could.

I model my teaching a lot on Dad's methods. He was always so patient in explaining detail, and, if I didn't understand something, he would demonstrate in a hands-on way whatever I was having a hard time grasping. He knew that real-life examples help children relate to the point being made. I've been able to do the same thing. As an example, I recently had to deal with a second-grade student who had pushed a young girl up against a wall at school, held her arms out against the wall, and kissed her. When I talked to the boy who had done this, I realized that he saw nothing wrong in this behavior. He wasn't trying to be bad. He just didn't understand the concept of respect. So I set out to try and explain how it was wrong to have forced the girl to accept his kiss.

I told him, "When you kissed Laura, it was just like you were stealing something. Has anyone ever taken something from you?"

"Yes, Miss," he replied, "I had some tennis shoes once that somebody took."

"Well, how did you feel when they took your shoes?" I asked.

"I didn't like it," he said.

"Well," I said, "that's probably just how Laura felt when you stole her kiss. That wasn't your kiss to steal."

"You mean like I took something that wasn't mine?" he asked.

"That's exactly what I mean," I said.

Tying the kiss into stolen tennis shoes is a bit of a stretch, but it helped him understand how Laura was feeling, and so it was important. I've found that when a student begins to understand how other people feel, it's usually harder for them to treat others badly.

Dad's idea of discipline has been valuable to me both as a person and as a teacher. It's important that you understand what I mean by "discipline." It's the behavioral environment established in a classroom, where it is important to maintain a sense of proportion and of fairness. A child's actions may be simply an acting-out of an issue with which he or she is trying to deal rather than an attempt to disrupt or disobey.

After all, one of the ways that people learn—about life as well as about academics—is by making mistakes. I believe teachers should not only allow but *encourage* students to make an attempt, even if in so doing, they might make a mistake. Since making a mistake is, after all, simply finding out what a certain boundary is, a teacher's or parent's response should be geared to appreciating the attempt the child has made, not keying on the failure.

I went through a time of real burn-out in my career, when I questioned everything that I was doing and whether I could keep on doing it. I would find myself saying things like, "The students don't really care. They're not planning their work. They're always tired or acting as if they're bored. I just can't go on." But then I put into practice one of Dad's techniques. I did a self-evaluation sheet and found out that *I* was the one who didn't really care. *I* was the one who was tired and bored. *I* was the one not doing enough planning. *I* was the problem. That brought me to the realization of how true it is that a teacher sets the tone for the classroom. When my attitude changed, so did the performance and attitude of the students.

I was so motivated by what I found out during that difficult time that I went back to school to get a counseling degree, so that I would be better able to help the special-education students for whom I am responsible. I wanted better tools to help me delve into the background of my students. I guess by then I had realized what a treasure I had been given in having been raised in a nurturing, loving home. It's such a far cry from the situations that many of my students experience that it's given me a desire to become more attuned to what they are feeling and struggling to contend with each day.

Another of the principles that has affected my adult life was Mom and Dad's insistence on doing the right thing. This actually cost me a job one time, when I was at a school where the principal had been literally run off by some of the policies in place. I, along with twenty-five of my thirty-two colleagues, resigned in protest. None of us wanted to leave, but we felt a need to support the principal, and a greater need to support a principle we thought was right. When I was explaining to my fifth-grade students that I would be leaving the school even though I didn't want to, I told them that I was going to continue teaching because I believed that it was the right thing to do, the thing I thought God wanted me to do, but that it would be at another school. The next day, one of my learning-disabled students gave me a note, which said, "Dear Miss, I'm glad God let you know what you were supposed to do." Responses like this make sacrificing for principles less difficult.

Dad's philosophy of doing the best with what you have has really paid off for me. Early in my career I was assigned to teach a special-education class out in the country. The students were aged from fourteen to twenty-one, and I had almost no materials with which to work. We had two carrels in the classroom, as well as two tables and some chairs, and that was about all. But it forced me to use creativity in planning my lessons, and it forced me to plan in great detail, using whatever I could to help me. My interest in football cards helped, since I used the cards to teach data-gathering skills and to hone reading skills. It's amazing what you can do when you're challenged.

Mom and Dad had never demanded that I get good grades as a student. They simply told me to do my best. But I put a lot of pressure on myself because I knew my parents had certain expectations of me and I wanted to meet them. I think it's very important to expect a lot from all students. That way, you give them the message that you think they are valuable. Of course, you have to tailor your expectations to their capabilities, but having low expectations of students tells them they have no worth in your eyes.

EPILOGUE by Tracy Teaff

Several situations come to mind that exemplify what Dad has taught me. My father has a very positive attitude, and this was obvious even when my house was flooded several years ago. The water rose to four and a half feet inside the house, leaving in its wake two and a half inches of mud. When it was time to evacuate the house, I called Dad, who said he'd be there as soon as he could. When he arrived, the waters had dropped a lot, and, characteristically, his first comment was, "Oh, Tracy, this is not so bad." But then he walked through the house to the back door, and saw the damage inside and out, where the deck had washed half-way around the house. He turned around with big old tears in his eyes and said, "I didn't realize how bad it was." But then, within a few seconds, he said, "Well, let's get on with cleaning this mess up. I bet it'll be prettier than it's ever been when we're finished." We hosed down the walls and floors, and Dad even cleaned out the air-conditioning compressors with a spoon. And you know what? It did turn out prettier than it had ever been.

Dad's practice of developing successful habits has been very helpful to me in teaching special-education children. It's so important for any teacher, but particularly a special-education teacher, to be consistent, to clearly define expectations, and to plan well. Students need to experience consistency daily and to know what kind of behavior is expected of them. These things affect not only the students' productivity and discipline in the classroom, but also the teacher's sanity.

As I began thinking about this epilogue, I was moved by the realization of how deeply entwined Dad's techniques are in my life and my teaching. Almost everything I do is rooted in his principles and beliefs. Dad's methods have worked for him, for thousands of players and coaches with whom he has worked or to whom he has spoken, and now they're working for me. I hope you can take some of the contents of this book, add it to your knowledge and expertise, then apply it in the classroom. Students will then be the beneficiaries of coaching in the classroom.

APPENDIX

Renaissance The reference to this program came from teacher Wally Green of Las Cruces, New Mexico. Grant Teaff has no further information about this program, and its mention should not be seen as an endorsement. It is included in the text for the purpose of informing other teachers.

MESA The reference to this program came from teacher David Griego of Mora, New Mexico. Grant Teaff has no further information about this program, and its mention should not be seen as an endorsement. It is included in the text for the purpose of informing other teachers.

VICA The reference to this program came from Doug Webster of Charlotte, Vermont. Grant Teaff has no further information about this program, and its mention should not be seen as an endorsement. It is included in the text for the purpose of informing teachers.

FHA The reference to this program came from Cindy Witt, of Mt. Vernon, Kentucky. GrantTeaff has no further information about this program, and its mention should not be seen as an endorsement. It is included in the text for the purpose of informing teachers.

AVID The reference to this program came from Joyce Pinkard of Madera, California. Grant Teaff has no further information about this program, and its mention should not be seen as an endorsement. It is included in the text for the purpose of informing teachers.